PRAISE FOR *GOD IS IN THE CITY*

"This is more than a collection of stories that describe the joys that go with the demands of urban ministry. It is a glimpse into how God is working to do extraordinary things through seemingly ordinary people, and how, through their efforts, there has been spiritual growth and increasing optimism concerning the future of the city."

TONY CAMPOLO, Professor Emeritus, Eastern University

"The world is changing rapidly like never before and Shawn Casselberry is the prophetic voice needed for times like these. *God is in the City* is a reminder to all of us connected to the church of not only our responsibility to the city but this book also reminds us of how much we can learn from the lives of people who live in the tension of struggle and grace daily. *God is in the City* gave me a new sense of hope."

RUDY RASMUS, Pastor at St. John's Downtown in Houston Texas and author of *Love.Period.-When All Else Fails*

"In these days of so much violence, blaming of poor and immigrants, disparities and hopelessness about our inner city communities, it is refreshing and encouraging to share these glimpses into the life and possibilities that Shawn shares in this book. He shares as an insider, his life is a testament of faith to that hope and action, and these stories, almost lyrical at times, are a reminder of God's presence, of the possibilities and the future. We can indeed, through this book, put on a new set of eyeglasses and look in a new way. Hopefully, we will be moved, as people of faith, to act for justice and community with these new insights."

MARY NELSON, Executive Director, Council for the Parliament of the World's Religions, and President Emeritus, Bethel New Life, Inc.

"In the spirit of Sara Miles' 'City of God,' and guided by the example offered by Jesus in the Gospels, Shawn Casselberry offers a powerful narrative lens through which we can see the world around us with fresh eyes and an open heart. His personal style transcends theological categorization, and his earnest willingness to be changed by the world he engages calls us to a similar kind of inspired, humble transformation."

CHRISTIAN PIATT, Author of *postChristian* and creator of the *Banned Questions* book series

"Shawn Casselberry has respectfully shared genuine stories and reflections that reveal both the glory and brokenness in our cities. *God is in the City* is a great introduction for all who seek a true understanding and honest reflection on God's work in the city and a great resource for those of us who have and will struggle living in the City's beautiful tension."

JONATHAN E.L. BROOKS, Senior Pastor, Canaan Community Church

"Shawn Casselberry has woven a rich tapestry that offers a glimpse of what God is up to in the city. More importantly, he teaches readers how to see people--right where they live--the way Good sees people."

MARGOT STARBUCK, author of *Small Things With Great Love:*
Adventures in Loving Your Neighbor

"Shawn has found a way to break open the walls we've built around our cities and bear to us the sacred ground that awaits us, challenging us to open our hearts and minds to the multitudes of the good and the bad within a city. Encouraging us to leave pre-conceived notions of terms like 'urban' and 'poverty' aside, he invites us to see things differently and be transformed by building human relationships grounded in an authentic love for all."

JOLLEEN WAGNER, Director of Lasallian Volunteers

"Shawn Casselberry's book is a testimony to the gospel truth that a person can save his life by losing it. With simple, moving stories of people who plunge into the messiness of urban life and discover God's presence there, he bears witness to God's power to transform us when we least expect it."

DEBORAH KAPP, Edward F and Phyllis K Campbell Associate Professor of Urban Ministry
at McCormick Theological Seminary

"Through *God is in the City*, Shawn uses the art of storytelling to convey the powerful message that God is still moving in the lives of people and specifically in those places where people are often forgotten. He provides a counter narrative to stereotypes and misconceptions drawn by those who have a negative opinion of poor urban communities. Like the Gospel, *God is in the City* tells stories of hope and liberation. Through his creative writing style, Shawn lets the stories speak for themselves as the reader hears the voice of God compelling us to go outside the walls of church buildings to reach the people nobody else seems to want. I'm grateful to Shawn for showing us what happens when God touches the lives of people in the city who want to know if God cares about them too."

ROMAL TUNE, Author of *God's Graffiti: Inspiring Stories for Teens*
www.RomalTune.com

"Shawn Casselberry is a leader of our times who writes from a deep place of compassion for friends and neighbors. His love for people shows in the way he sees beauty in each situation. Shawn's life and words are a breath of fresh air in these challenging times."

"Across the planet, cities are increasing at an unprecedented rate. Masses of humanity pour in seeking a measure of prosperity, connection, and communality. Too often however, they find only disappointment, loneliness, brokenness, and pain. Cities can be a harsh place. But that doesn't tell the whole story. Cities can also be a source of hope and promise. Shawn Casselberry mixes his personal experiences in the urban streets of Chicago with engaging stories of urban dwellers as they encounter the ups and downs, the give and take of city life. In *God is in the City,* Casselberry captures the truth that God walks among the city's inhabitants, even in the darkest of alleyways and the most brightly lit thoroughfares. This is good news."

"Shawn Casselberry has a deep love for God and people – especially those living in the big city. His love is broken open in his writing, illuminating his efforts to be faithful to a God present in all things and all places. Shawn challenges us to be aware of and embrace the myriad moments God is embodied in life and in the city.

"*God is in the City* is a much needed book as it will give narrative to the ongoing struggle it is to live in today's U.S. urban spaces, Shawn locates the heart of issues by using narrative to tell that story. The library of urban ministry just got larger in a very good way. Get this read and learn from the experiences and people that make up our cities and hear what God is up to.

"Shawn lives an authentic life, rubbing shoulders with real people from every walk of life. He has humbly allowed these encounters to transform him. In *God is in the City*, his engaging storytelling exalts the city's true beauty and acknowledges her real pain. He offers an open-handed invitation for readers to fall in love with the city and her people."

SARAH QUEZADA, writer and blogger at A Life with Subtitles
www.alifewithsubtitles.com

"Shawn Casselberry's *God is in the City* invites us to find new images of the sacred and the divine in places we might usually avoid. He challenges our familiar ways of imaging God and opens our eyes to unexpected sacraments and encounters with God in what might seem some of the most unlikely places. In a frenzied world, these stories remind us to slow down, pay attention, look and see."

CAZ TOD-PEARSON, Executive Director, The Simple Way
and National Program Director for Mission Year

"With pages full of grace and hope, Shawn weaves a tapestry of reminders that God is in the city. I have seen firsthand Shawn's passion for opening people's eyes to the divine in the midst of the ordinary. This book is full of stories that will inspire and encourage a deep commitment to becoming more aware of the ways God is at work around you."

JASON SHAFFER, Area Coordinator, Calvin College

"After more than 10 years in Chicago, Shawn testifies beautifully to the transforming power of the city – which I personally experienced over a 10 week period during seminary. When life is immersed in the city like that of he and his wife – the strength, beauty, and hope of people and neighborhoods becomes visible. While we've understood global missions to have suffered from poor missiology up into the 20th century, *God is in the City* is a gift to see people answering the call to Urban America – while embracing missiology that engages relationships, culture, and struggle. In many marginalized neighborhoods in the city, the Spirit of God is at work, and this book brings to light terrific stories of redemption in places that had known years of brokenness."

REV. GREG HASELOFF, Campus Chaplain of Asbury University

Lizo,
od is in the far Northwest!.
Be a witness for God's
peace & justice!

God is in the City

Encounters of Grace and Transformation

Shawn Casselberry

Foreword by John Perkins

This book is dedicated to the Chicago neighborhoods of East Garfield Park, North Lawndale, La Villita, Englewood, and Roseland and the heroic leaders and organizations that are working every day to bring hope and lasting change to the city.

Some of the names in this book have been changed to show respect for the individuals and their stories.

All proceeds of this book will go to Mission Year's continued work in cities across the country.

To join or support Mission Year go to: www.missionyear.org

Mission Year Life Resources is an initiative of Mission Year to provide tools for individuals and churches to love God and love people in whatever community God has placed them.

ISBN: 1501021869
ISBN-13: 978-1501021862

Library of Congress Control Number: 2014916899
Printed in Charleston, SC

"God is in the midst of the city; it shall not be moved;
God will help it when the morning dawns."

- Psalm 46:5 *NRSV*

CONTENTS

FOREWORD

BY JOHN PERKINS

We live in a time of tremendous challenge. We live in a world of unprecedented wealth, yet we have unparalleled inequality. We live in a nation that believes in "liberty and justice for all," yet we have more people incarcerated than any other nation in the world. We attend churches that proclaim a gospel of reconciliation, yet Sunday morning is still the most segregated hour in America. Our cities are full of challenges too – poverty, injustice, segregation and violence. It's enough to make one lose heart.

But I still have hope.

I have hope because – as this book so beautifully states – God is in the city. God is touching the hearts and minds of people, young and old, to bear witness to the love of God in every neighborhood. These stories of grace and transformation give me hope that God is up to more than we could ever imagine.

God has not abandoned the city. God has not forsaken the poor.

God is a God of justice who hears and responds to the cries of the oppressed. Shawn Casselberry is someone who has taken the time to look and listen where God is working in the city. He doesn't ignore the great challenges, but shows us how God is present in the midst of them to bring good from even the most heartbreaking situations.

God is in the City is an inspiring collection of personal stories and prophetic insights that guide us to see the city and God with new eyes. Through moving stories from Shawn's personal experience living and working in cities across the country, Shawn draws our attention to the places and people where we can find God alive and active. While poverty, violence, and injustice abound in America's urban areas, Shawn shows us there is also deep faith, authentic community, and courageous struggle. Whereas, urban communities are often viewed negatively, or one-dimensionally in the media and also in the church, Shawn shows us how the city is a sacrament capable of transforming us. In fact, if you haven't experienced God in the city, you might be missing out on experiencing a big part of God's heart.

This book invites us to enter into the beauty and struggle, to see where God's promise and purpose are breaking through in messy, mundane, and miraculous moments of life. With passion and hope, Shawn recounts the many ways God is in the city.

I urge you to read this book. You will be inspired and transformed by what you encounter. Most importantly, you will be challenged and equipped to be a witness of God's love in your own neighborhood and city. The greatest task for those who live in the city, as well as those from the outside who choose to join alongside of those already there, is to find a way to help the hurting people without victimizing them further and causing the problem to grow. We still struggle with this even though we are learning to do it better. We need deeper reconciliation across ethnic barriers. We must love each other well enough that we can share in each other's pain, while also empowering those who have been victimized. Right now, we struggle to have that conversation, but it is only through the deep empathy and love, modeled in the life, death, and resurrection of Jesus Christ, who was "pierced for our transgression and crushed for our iniquities" that we can come together in a real way and experience true reconciliation and peace between all people.

I have devoted the rest of my life to pouring into emerging leaders like the young people in Mission Year and urban communities across the country. I am inspired by this new generation of young people that desire to plant and develop more multicultural communities. I hope you too will enter into this beautiful, heartbreaking, and transformational movement of God in the city. As someone who has spent the last fifty-seven of my eighty-four years in this work, I can say with confidence: You will not regret it!

DR. JOHN M. PERKINS
Founder of the John M. and Vera Mae Perkins Foundation
Co-founder of the Christian Community Development Association
Lives with his wife of sixty-three years, Vera Mae, in Jackson, Mississippi

INTRODUCTION

GOD IS IN THE CITY:
DEVELOPING EYES TO SEE

"Conversion is not implanting eyes, for they exist already; but giving them a right direction, which they have not."
- Plato

"The real voyage of discovery consists not in seeking new landscapes, but in having new eyes."
- Marcel Proust

God is in the city, which means the city can be a sacrament of grace and transformation. Because God is in all things, God can be encountered in all places, all moments, and all people. Our role in the city is not to save or fix the city, but to allow ourselves to be changed alongside those we come to serve. By developing eyes to see God in the city, even the places of deep pain and injustice can become opportunities to encounter God's grace and transformation.

"The life of our city is rich in poetic and marvelous subjects. We are enveloped and steeped as though in an atmosphere of the marvelous; but we do not notice it."

- Charles Baudelaire

God is in the city. God was here before I got here. God will be here long after I'm gone.

I have encountered God in the city in ways I could not have anticipated. I relocated to the city in response to a call. A physical phone call for a job offer for my wife and me to work with Mission Year, and a two-year inner calling I felt to move to the city after reading John Perkins' book *Restoring At-risk Communities*. I wanted to do something about the pain and injustice I had learned was deeply embedded in our country's urban cities. I wanted to contribute. I wanted to be a light. You know, all the things us Christian do-gooders want to do. After a decade of living and working in the city, I can honestly say the city has done more for me than I have done for it. In actuality, the city has done something to me.

I have been changed inalterably. I have been transformed by the city, the neighborhoods, and the people I've met in urban communities across the country. I have been transformed by God through the grace I've encountered in the city.

Most people tend to see the city as either a trendy, hip place to be or a crime-ridden, hopeless place to avoid. In reality, the city is both a place of extreme wealth and debilitating poverty, progressive change and systemic injustice, eternal hope and crushing despair. It can largely depend on which side of the city you visit or happen to live.

For the last decade I have lived in Chicago. A beautiful, historic American city. We are known as "the city that works." We have a world-class public transit system, breathtaking skyline, picturesque parks and museums, competitive sports teams, and rich cultural diversity. Yet we are also known for political corruption, failing schools, high violence, and the notorious distinction of being the most racially segregated city in America.[1] Living and working in North Lawndale on the west side of Chicago, an area known for concentrated poverty, violence, unemployment, and addiction, gives me the chance to see the parts of the city that don't work.

Seeing these grim realities has led me to ask the question, "Where is God in the city?" Sure, we can imagine seeing God in the developed downtown areas, lakefronts, and nature preserves where, "God is good!" so effortlessly slips off the tongue. But can God also be experienced in the neglected parts of the city where God's goodness may be more in doubt? How do we see God in the brokenness and struggle of communities plagued with poverty and injustice? How do we not grow cynical and hopeless in light of the historic injustices we see in cities across America? How can we proclaim the Good News when most of the news we hear about the city seems more like bad news?

Too often, news outlets give us a daily rundown of crimes across the city's struggling areas without reporting any of the good that is going on in those neighborhoods. We get raw, cold information without any interpretative framework for making sense of the sorrow and with no sign of any hope on the horizon. Many people, both religious and nonreligious, are unable to process this tragedy, violence, and injustice, much less see hope in the midst of it all.

Instead of ignoring these uncomfortable aspects of our cities and society, we can look at them with new eyes. We can see where grace may be present under the surface, on the margins, in the background, and sometimes right in front of our faces. Developing new eyes helps us to see potential where others only see problems. We see that God is in the city - and if God is in the city, the city is not just a place of contradictions and challenges; it is a sacrament of grace and transformation.[2]

As I have lived and been involved in ministry in the city over the last decade, I have encountered God in many places and through many people. This book is a personal collection of stories and recollection of moments of encountering God's grace in the midst of the challenges of urban life.

I didn't always know God could be encountered in this way. When I first came to the city it felt as if I were going to an abandoned place. I was nervous and unsure. Having lived most of my life in small towns and rural areas, I arrived with fear and anxiety about living in an historically marginalized community. I had spent the previous three years in seminary in rural Kentucky, deconstructing the faith handed down to me. I desired to have a faith radical enough to follow Jesus – particularly across the racial and economic barriers that divided me from so many others. I had all but lost faith in the Church being any kind of reconciling agent, while desperately wanting to be proven wrong.

Although I felt called to the city, that didn't make the entry any easier. At first, I did not feel God's presence at all. It wasn't until I had a very real encounter with God in the city that my whole perspective changed. I remember very vividly staying up late one night in my apartment with a candle lit on the end table next to the couch. I was sitting quietly in the darkness reflecting, journaling, and trying to pray. Unexpectedly, I was awakened to God's presence in the room in a way I had not felt before. I had a sudden awareness that God was there. All my fears departed. I was not in a place forsaken by God, but in a place where God wanted to meet me and show me the grace that already existed there.

Initially, I thought I was called to the city to serve and help, and of course I try to do that, but I now understand that I was invited to encounter God in the city, in the neighborhood, in the people, and even in myself — to discover, as the Jesuits say, that God is in all things. The same grace that works to redeem me is also working within the city.

When I left my house the next day everything was different. I started seeing that God was all around me. Like Jacob who declared, "Surely the LORD is in this place and I didn't know it,"[3] I started to recognize God and grace everywhere I went, often in unexpected places and people. I began to see the city as a sacrament of grace and transformation, and it changed everything.

I developed eyes of grace. And that is the great challenge for all of us – to learn to see. To be able to see that God is in our cities, no matter the size of the city or in which side of town we live. As individuals and as communities, urban ministers and suburbanites, we need vision. We need to see. I believe the greatest tragedy would be to have the kingdom of God in our midst and fail to see it. Tragically, this is exactly what happens over and over throughout history.

God is in the City is about ordinary, and sometimes extra-ordinary, encounters in which grace and transformation break through the mundane, messy moments of life. This book is not about any great deeds we can do for the city, but about letting ourselves be changed by God's presence in the city. This might seem like a new way to think about our relationship to the city, but look at the story of Peter and Cornelius in Acts 10. Peter receives a call to visit Cornelius in the city. Cornelius is a Gentile. Peter has no room in his heart or theology for Gentiles at this point in his life and truly wants nothing to do with them. God gives him a vision – gives him eyes to see – that God's grace is bigger, wider than he originally thought. God's grace extends equally to Gentiles. God sends Peter to Cornelius not only so Cornelius (and his household) can experience this grace, but so Peter can be changed, too. That is how God works. God sends us to other people so we can be transformed together. Urban ministry is about joining in where God is at work and allowing ourselves to be changed alongside those we come to serve. As we embrace God's presence in the city, the city changes us. Like Peter, sometimes we have to be changed in order to change the world.

My hope with this book is that you will start to see all the moments of your life, both the miraculous and monotonous, as opportunities for divine encounters of grace and transformation. I hope that through these experiences and stories, you will look at things differently. You will see how God is present in the city and in everyday people, places, and events. I hope you will be inspired, challenged, comforted, and at times disturbed by what you see. I hope you will see urban communities as they are: full of people with heroic faith who courageously struggle against forces of evil and injustice. They are God's children who have much to teach us. I hope you will see God with new eyes. God is not distant or outside of our everyday experiences, but accessible and ever-present, ready to be encountered in the city.

I hope you'll recognize God is with you as you commute to work, rest in a park, protest against injustice, or pray by candlelight in your favorite armchair.

God is in your city. God was there before you got there. God will be there long after you are gone.

CHAPTER ONE

BAPTIZED BY FIRE HYDRANT:
ENCOUNTERS OF GRACE AND LOVE

"I do not at all understand the mystery of grace - only that it meets us where we are but does not leave us where it found us."
- Anne Lamott

The city brings us face to face with the necessity and complexity of grace in our journey of faith. Entering into the city is like a baptism. We are transformed by grace as we fully enter into the joys and struggles of our neighbors. As we grasp grace for ourselves, we are able to fall in love with God and the communities we are called to serve, to live lives of gratitude, and to stretch the limits of our grace for others.

Baptism by Fire Hydrant

"Sacraments are like hoses. They are channels of the living water of God's grace. Our faith is like opening the faucet. We can open it a lot, a little, or not at all."

- Peter Kreeft

I was baptized in the streets of Chicago.

Chicago is known for being cold, but it is as hot in the summer as it is cold in the winter. In the scorching summers, many die from the heat. The Chicago Tribune recently reported, "Soaring heat kills more people a year than hurricanes, lightning, tornadoes, floods, and earthquakes combined."[1] Many of my neighbors do not have air conditioning in their homes. I've been in apartments where the thermostat has registered as high as 105 degrees. This is why many seek refuge from the heat on front porches or in the shade of trees outside.

On especially hot days, a neighborhood hero will come along and open a fire hydrant. This is one of the unexpected joys one might even call a city sacrament. All it takes to create a water park on a city street are two simple objects: a piece of wood and an old tire. The tire is placed around the hydrant and the wooden plank is stuffed into the tire so that when the water is released it sprays upward in an arc that covers the street. When the hydrant is opened, kids run from blocks away to immerse themselves in the water. It is a relief from the oppressive heat and creates an oasis in the desert.

I remember my first experience with a fire hydrant in the city. I was sweating through my shirt due to the heat. I heard that a fire hydrant had been opened down the street so I followed the crowds of kids that flocked toward it. There were already children laughing and playing in the puddles. I was tentative at first, not sure how powerful the water would be. I reached out and touched the waterfall with my fingers. It was so cold and refreshing. I desperately wanted to go in but I worried about my clothes getting drenched and walking around wet the rest of the afternoon. I wondered what people would think of me.

Here I was, a white seminary-educated male in my late twenties, standing on the sidewalk, internally debating whether I would join in. As an outsider, I wondered if I would be accepted by the neighborhood where we were placing ourselves. As a white Christian male, I wondered if I could prove that I was different than the other whites, the other Christians, and the other males who have wreaked a lot of havoc in the name of God. I doubted whether a seminary grad from rural Kentucky would ever be able to relate and build meaningful relationships with people who, on the surface, appeared so different from me. I fought inner doubts that said, "What are you doing here? You don't belong here! Why don't you just go back to Kentucky!" It's funny, looking back. This moment seemed frozen in time. What was probably only a 15-30 second pause felt like it lasted for hours. For some reason, it felt like a lot was riding on this decision. Would I choose to stay separated from the community by fear and doubt, or would I join in by taking a leap of faith? It was a crucial moment of decision.

After a few moments of internal debate, I decided to go for it. I knew I couldn't just observe from the sidelines. I didn't want to miss out on this divine moment. So I lowered my head and stepped into the heart of the hydrant's flow. The hydrant released gallons of water each minute that streamed up into the air and crashed down on the street below. I braced myself for the impact. The water came rushing down all over me, instantly soaking my hair, my shirt, and my pants. I was completely drenched. My whole body felt the sensation of ice-cold streams. I felt alive. Refreshed. Renewed. Children were watching me with curiosity and laughing. I laughed and played like a child, totally free. I stomped around in the puddles, not caring what I looked like or who saw me.

I knew in that moment my life had changed forever. I had been washed head to toe. I had been converted. From across the street, the Pentecostal church that I could barely make out through the waves of water pouring down provided witness to the transformation. I would never return to the life of fear, prejudice, and segregation I had known before. My allegiance was no longer to a white American cultural Christianity. I was following the Spirit of Jesus into a new place that actually required me to trust beyond what I knew. I was being initiated into a new kingdom and a new community that required new eyes.

I went in an observer, an outsider to the neighborhood, and I emerged a member of the community. I realized that fully entering into the daily experiences of my neighbors is a grace. It is baptism, a way of becoming part of a new community. You can't become part of the neighborhood if you are not willing to enter into the joys and struggles of your neighbors. I joined in.

Family Matters

"You don't choose your family. They are God's gift to you, as you are to them."
- Desmond Tutu

After feeling the call to relocate to the west side of Chicago, I did what anyone else would do – I called my mom. My mom is a prayer warrior and I trust her guidance more than anyone's. I told her about our decision to move into North Lawndale. I told her we felt good about the decision and that we were sensing God was in it. I was expecting confirmation. Since she was so close to God, I figured God would naturally let her in on the plan. Instead, my mom had reservations. She did not feel right about it.

This led to a major internal crisis. Do I follow the advice of my mom who I respect and trust or do I heed the voice inside urging me onward? I went against my mom's premonition and followed what my wife and I sensed God leading us to do.

The first six months in the neighborhood was tough. Our car was broken into. We struggled to get to know people at church and in the community. We both experienced anxiety and fear. It was difficult. We second-guessed ourselves. We second-guessed God.

We did not want to admit defeat but we felt pretty defeated. We thought we must have heard God wrong. But something kept us from giving up. We decided that we would take advantage of every opportunity and give it one last try. If it didn't work out, at least it wouldn't be because we didn't give our all.

We dove into the activities at our church. One thing led to another and, within a week, we found ourselves with opportunities to plug into the church and neighborhood. Two guys in particular, Stanley and Willie, embraced me and helped me put my passion for drums to use. They invited me to play with the church praise band and help out with a community drumline with kids who have incarcerated loved ones. The Frederick Buechner quote, "the place God calls you is the place where your deep gladness and the world's deep hunger meet," was coming to life.[2] I loved drumline in high school and never thought I would be involved in a drumline again. I had started to believe that serving God in the city would inevitably be miserable. But in this one week I felt Willie and Stanley had reached inside me, pulled out my passions and given me purpose. My heart was overwhelmed by the grace of it.

The next day was Martin Luther King Sunday. I had been up all night, my mind racing. I felt so much gratitude and grace. Secretly, I had felt like I did not deserve to be accepted in the community because I was white. I felt like I had to prove myself to earn the respect of the community. I had to work extra hard to compensate for all the oppression that had been done to African Americans over so many years by people of my hue. But those kinds of scars cannot be healed by any amount of work or effort on the part of even the most eager white person. My only hope was to be shown grace, a grace that I didn't deserve. When Willie and Stanley extended friendship to me, it opened the floodgates and I was transformed by grace. I could no longer serve out of guilt or fear. I was freed to love.

During our church service, there is a time for prayer and praise. I knew that I would have to testify or my heart would explode.

I stood in line and approached the microphone when it was my turn. While sharing all that God had done, I broke down in tears. I shared about how those two guys reached out to me and how their grace had changed me. After the service, we were surrounded by people who asked for our phone numbers and who wanted to meet up. One of the church leaders pulled me aside and ended up becoming my North Lawndale mom. I began to get involved with her family and she became involved in mine. I was adopted into the family of God, and it felt so good to belong.

We had toiled and strived on our own for six months with no results. I think sometimes God waits for us to come to the end of our own strength. It's as if God is standing there asking, "Are you done yet? You ready for me to step in?" In a moment of grace, everything had changed. We had a home, a family, a community, and a purpose.

I thought my strength and resolve would enable me to become accepted into the community. Thinking back on it now, it turned out to be my weakness. My brokenness. My tears. Although I had been attending the church for six months, it wasn't until that Sunday that we were fully seen and embraced. Ironically, some people still tell me they remember my "first" Sunday when I got up and spoke.

Later my mom visited me in Chicago. I took her to church and around the neighborhood to meet my Lawndale family. Afterwards, she looked at me sincerely and said, "You are right where you need to be."

Falling in Love

"Things are beautiful if you love them."
- Mother Teresa

Working for Mission Year – a national Christian ministry for young adults focused on faith, community, and social justice – has given me opportunities to see God working in cities across the country and even the world. During a trip to Buenos Aires, Argentina, I met with a local Argentine pastor who shared something very profound with me. In regards to folks entering a new city he said, simply and succinctly, that they need to "fall in love."

I was stunned. He summarized the goal of missions in three words! Although I have a seminary degree in missions and have worked in a mission organization for years, I have never heard anyone describe missions as falling in love. But when he said it, I was struck by the beauty and wisdom behind the statement.

What he meant was people called to Argentina need to fall in love with Argentina. People called to India have to fall in love with India. People called to the city have to fall in love with the city. Ministry is not about pushing our own agendas. It is all about falling in love. The world is redeemed by love.

When I came back from Argentina I shared this idea of falling in love with our Mission Year staff and teams. We incorporated this as our approach to the communities and people we serve. Before, I would say we are here to serve or to make a difference, but now I say we are here to fall in love. When we fall in love, we see things differently. To fall in love is to see the beauty and brokenness, strength and struggle, and to be captivated by it all.

You cannot make it happen, but you can know when it does. When you fall in love, the whole landscape is transformed. You see beauty in the people and the place and all you want to do is behold it. You want to be one with it. You want communion.

Falling in love with a city is a lot like falling in love with a person. It is easy to be infatuated and to remain on a superficial level. Most people are infatuated with the city. We may like certain parts of the city, like the trendy touristy areas downtown or the shopping and entertainment districts. When I tell people I am from Chicago, they usually say, "I love Chicago!" Then I ask what parts they have been to and inevitably they say, "You know, Michigan Avenue and downtown." If that is all you have seen of the city, you are only infatuated.

To fall in love means to see the city more intimately, to see the parts that not everyone gets a chance to see or takes the time to see. Most people see and stay in the wealthy parts of the city, avoiding economically struggling areas or even labeling whole areas as "the bad part of town." Only after seeing both sides of a city, the poverty and the prosperity, can you say you are in love with the city. When you love something, you want to know all of it.

When I am in other cities, I try to make a point to visit the economically struggling parts of the city as well as the tourist sites. I want a more accurate picture of the city. I want to know the struggles and triumphs of the city, the places of suffering and celebration. I want to fully experience and embrace the city. Jesus fell in love with the city. In a remarkable passage, Jesus weeps over the city of Jerusalem, crying out, "How often I have longed to gather your children together, like a hen gathers her chicks under her wings."[3] Falling in love with a city means you will suffer for the city's redemption and you will commit your life to its betterment.

When I first came to the city I was infatuated. I was not sure I wanted to commit. We would take it one year at a time. We were dating, I guess you would say. After about five years, we finally said, "I can see us being here for a long time."

Am I still dating? 2/16/15

After experiencing the different sides of the city and planting ourselves in a neighborhood most people drive around to avoid, we fell in love. We got involved with youth in the neighborhood with incarcerated loved ones through a music program that seeks to be a family for those whose families have been torn apart by the prison system. We got to see how gifted the kids were and learn more about the struggles they endure. We saw how the leaders of the program, who grew up in the neighborhood, would weep over the situations the kids were going through and how they extended themselves to support them.

One day I was sitting with one of the founders of the program, Antoinette, as she talked about the challenges the kids face growing up in the neighborhood. She was referring to the poor schools, the gangs and violence, the abuse, and the uphill battle they face trying to get out of poverty. With tears in her eyes she said,

"They are all my kids." And they were. She fought as hard for the kids in her neighborhood as she fought for her own kids.

We started seeing that there was grace, beauty, community, and hope in the midst of pain and struggle. We learned from people like Antoinette and her husband Stanley, what it really means to fall in love with the community. After witnessing this kind of commitment from so many saints in the neighborhood, we decided to commit, and put our roots down in this place. We bought a house and this neighborhood and city are now home. It is not always easy, but love has a way of lifting you and making hard things lighter. What someone could never make you do, you do gladly for love.

When I asked one of our volunteers in Philadelphia what she thought of the city after being there for a few months she said, "There's trash and broken glass but there are also beautiful murals. There's crime and poverty but there's also rich community. I didn't expect it to be so beautiful." That's what it sounds like to fall in love.

Just yes.

Update: Stanley and Antoinette Ratliff

Stanley and Antoinette continue to live in North Lawndale and minister to families of the incarcerated through their nonprofit organization Celestial Ministries. Antoinette just wrote a book about her battle with breast cancer called, "A Test of Times." Stanley just received a Masters of Arts in Christian Ministries with an Urban Studies focus from Northern Theological Seminary. They have been married since 1992 and continue to love kids in the neighborhood like their own.

Spare Change

"We are beggars. This is true."
- Martin Luther

Being approached for money on the street is a common occurrence in the city. To be honest, I used to get tired of being asked. Sometimes I would inwardly cringe when someone approached me because I knew I was going to have to go through the whole internal battle of whether I was going to give or not. If I was going to give what was I going to give, and why I was giving it.

But then I started to see what a sacrament it is. Much like Communion invites you and me to examine our hearts in light of our need for grace, so does the encounter with the beggar lead us to examine our conscience.

The encounters have a way of unearthing the depths of us: Sometimes it is fear. We are afraid of those in need. Sometimes it is greed or stinginess. We don't want to share what we have with others. Sometimes it is impatience. We don't have the time. Sometimes it is distrust. We don't know what they will do with what we give. Sometimes it is indifference to the plight of others. We really don't care. When these things lay buried or hidden inside us, we can't see where WE may need change. What really troubles us about the beggar is that he/she makes us confront ourselves and our own poverty of generosity and compassion.

Mission Year hosts a Solidarity retreat where we invite churches and young adult groups to better understand the struggles of the homeless. We take them downtown without any money where they are asked to see how people treat them when they hold a cup and sign, beg for their lunch, and hang out the homeless. They don't have to beg, and many don't want to, but once they start getting hungry it's not too long before they are giving it a try.

Clay, who served in our yearlong program, had this experience as he spent the day on the streets of Chicago.[4]

"We each picked a partner and were told to head downtown and proceed to live as the homeless do. We were challenged to beg for money to buy lunch, to meet other homeless people downtown and to hear their stories. Let me tell you, many interesting experiences occurred during that day, one of which will most vividly remain in my mind.

I was sitting on the steps leading down to the subway train, asking people for money as they passed me by (most of whom ignored me, acted distracted, clutched their purses tightly, or pulled their children close to them); but one lady in particular I will never forget. As she was walking down the steps I asked if she would mind sparing 25 cents so that I could get lunch.

She turned and faced me, and then proceeded to say, 'What the hell is wrong with you? What is wrong with you? Can't you get a job? Why won't you work for your money?'

I responded by saying I was merely trying to get some lunch, seeing as I hadn't eaten all day and it was nearly 2:00 pm.

She then said, 'Well haven't you ever had a job? Oh, I bet I know what happened. You probably got fired for doing drugs or something didn't you? That's all you are is some drug addict aren't you?'

I responded by telling her that jobs were just hard to come by.

She then said, 'You're pathetic, just pathetic. (Then, reaching into her wallet, she pulled out a dollar.) I can't believe I'm giving this to you, because I know all you're going to spend it on is drugs or cigarettes,' and continued on her original path."

Proverbs says, "Those who mock the poor insult their Maker," and "whoever gives to the poor, lends to the LORD."[5] When we speak insults against the poor, we strip them of their dignity and we end up mocking God. People always ask if they should give money to the homeless. We want an easy answer to free us from the tension of grace. It's working through the tension that allows us to truly grow into compassionate people.

Clay's experience not only impacted him but also his family back home in Memphis. When his mom heard about how her son was treated, she was convicted. She realized her reactions to the homeless were more like the woman Clay encountered. She also realized that every homeless person is someone's son or daughter. Clay's parents decided to take action. They went downtown in their city and started spending time with the homeless there. Clay's dad even felt led to sell his dental practice to pursue full-time ministry to the homeless. From the simple grace of identifying with the homeless, a whole family has been moved into action. Recently, while visiting with Clay's parents over a meal in Chicago, we were approached by someone asking for money for food. Clay's dad instinctively got up and bought the gentleman lunch. Their lives reflect the grace of a God who gives generously and indiscriminately.

Now, I try to be prepared for the divine encounters. I bring a stash of granola bars, water bottles, or spare coins in my car or in my pockets when I know I might encounter someone. I settle in my heart what I want to give so I am not giving out of compulsion or guilt. Sometimes I don't give money. I just give a smile, wave, exchange names, or stop and talk for a while. I try to let the Spirit of grace lead me. I like carrying a resource card for a local shelter with numbers for various services around the city. Other times I fumble for words to say or miss out on the sacrament altogether.

In the end, the beggar shows us where we lack, which is a grace worth at least the spare change in our pockets.

Update: Clay Carson

After serving in the Englewood neighborhood in Chicago with Mission Year, Clay worked as an Area Director for K-Life and Youth Pastor in Enid, OK alongside his wife Katrina. In 2012, Clay moved back to Chicago to get a BA in Pastoral Ministry from Moody Bible Institute and serve as the children's and youth director for Free Church in Oak Park, IL. Clay will graduate this year and start a ministry leadership training program at Free Church.

Gratitude

"For me, every hour is grace."
- Elie Wiesel

A common prayer among those in our community is, "Thank you for waking me up this morning." At first glance, it may seem like a simple statement, but when you hear the stories of how God has sustained people in the midst of daily struggles you realize it comes out of a deep faith and gratitude. In communities where people are struggling to get by, nothing is taken for granted. Every day is welcomed as a gift of grace from a loving God. Life itself is seen as something for which to give God thanks.

Kaylyn shared about her experience living and going to church in Roseland, a neighborhood on Chicago's south side:

"I have experienced the uninhibited praise of people who are grateful for life, family, and God's provision. I have discovered a part of my Christianity (my true humanity) that up to this point in my life, has been greatly lacking if not absent all together: gratitude. As I have worshipped alongside my neighbors I have witnessed genuine thankfulness. The praise reports at prayer time at my church are often littered with phrases like, 'God provided money for a tank of gas' or 'I am just thankful I woke up this morning.' As a person coming from security and privilege, I take for granted the gift of another day, a job, food in the fridge, a good family, educational opportunities, and a safe place to live."

Quen, another Mission Year volunteer, grew up in a low-income household and did not receive a lot of privileges that many middle class folks take for granted. Yet, Quen has a spirituality of gratitude that is contagious. While others grumble or complain about inconveniences, Quen gives thanks. He does not feel thankful for everything that happens, but he finds something in every situation to be thankful for.

Have you ever noticed that those with the least material privileges seem to have the most gratitude? Coming from a place of material privilege, I have had to learn gratitude from my neighbors here in the city. Privilege can make us feel entitled to what we have rather than being thankful. We are not thankful because we believe we've earned what we have. We believe that what we have is a result of our own hard work and therefore exclusively ours to enjoy, rather than as a gift from God to be shared with others. Grace, in any of the forms it comes to us, whether physical or spiritual blessings, is always an unearned gift.

Spiritual writer Henri Nouwen realized his ingratitude after immersing himself among the economically poor in South America:

"What I claim as a right, my friends…received as a gift; what is obvious to me was a joyful surprise to them; what I take for granted, they celebrate in thanksgiving; what for me goes by unnoticed became for them a new occasion to say thanks. And slowly I learned. I learned what I must have forgotten somewhere in my busy, well-planned, and very 'useful' life. I learned that everything that is, is freely given by the God of love. All is grace. Light and water, shelter and food, work and free time, children, parents, and grandparents, birth and death – it is all given to us. Why? So that we can say gracias, thanks: thanks to God, thanks to each other, thanks to all and everyone."[6]

Anthony de Mello said, "You sanctify whatever you are grateful for." When we become grateful people, all our hours and moments become sacred.

Update: Kaylyn Moran

After serving in Mission Year in 2011, Kaylyn earned her Masters in Higher Education Administration from Georgia Southern and currently works as a Resident Director at Asbury University. Kaylyn is continuing to learn the practical application of 'loving your neighbor' as she lives in and leads a residence hall of 18-22 year old women. Her neighbors in Roseland helped her see each day as a gift and a new adventure in kingdom building.

Update : Quentin Darnell

Quen served his first Mission Year in the East Garfield Park neighborhood in Chicago 2011-2012 and then served a second year with Mission Year as an alumni leader in the Pittsburgh neighborhood in Atlanta 2012-2013. He is now living in Clarkston, GA in a community with a large refugee population. He is getting married this year and interested in pursuing international missions.

Limits of Grace

"Millions of hells of sinners cannot come near to exhaust infinite grace."
- Samuel Rutherford

There's a street preacher I see often standing outside the Gap Store downtown. He has an amplifier and microphone in which he screams incessantly about hell and condemnation of sin to all who walk by. I think this is the image many people have of God. An angry, judgmental man ready to condemn and cast people into hell.

But Jesus operated very differently. Jesus exemplified a life of grace and love. Every moment was intentional, pursuing God, seeing dignity in the person in front of him, being open to the ones in whom grace was needed most. Jesus seemed a lot less preoccupied with hell and who was going, and more concerned about who was missing out on grace and how he could show it to them. Jesus touched the very ones the rest of society labeled "unclean." Jesus extended grace to everyone around him, even to the ones who acted out violently against him. The cross reveals the limitless depths of God's love and grace. After being beaten and crucified unjustly, Christ is able to say to those who are murdering him, "Father forgive them, for they know not what they do."

The way of love for Jesus meant extending a radical grace to the world so that even his enemies would feel it. There is no individual or institution in the world that lives out such limitless grace (sadly, not even the church). As Christians, our great challenge is to reflect that kind of grace to the people in our cities that need it the most.

One of our Mission Year volunteers who worked at a Christian homeless shelter had to come to terms with the limits of his own grace. Justin developed a close relationship with Melvin*. Melvin was a story of transformation and hope for all the guys at the shelter. He was even featured as a success story on the organization's website! After months of commitment and dedication he was showing amazing signs of progress and improvement. That is, until it came to light that Melvin had been a sex offender. The facility welcomes homeless men, the unemployed, former drug addicts, and the formerly incarcerated, but it does not accept sex-offenders.

As a former teacher, Justin understands the damage sex-offenders cause children. He always felt a deep hatred for anyone that could cause harm to children. But now here was Melvin, someone he had gotten to know for the last six months. Melvin confessed he had not divulged the information, that it happened 13 years ago, that he deeply regretted it and that he himself had been sexually abused as a kid. During his time at the shelter he genuinely turned his life over to Christ and had become a new creation. Now Melvin was being kicked out onto the streets and Justin was wrestling with what Jesus would do. Even when institutions cannot show grace, what is our responsibility as Christians to the broken in our world? What are the limits of our grace?

Justin decided that his commitment to Christ meant going beyond the limits of his own grace and extending the limitless grace Jesus offers. He decided Christ would continue a relationship with Melvin and give grace as freely as he received it. He realized that he was as much a sinner as Melvin. The only difference was that his sin was not made public like Melvin's. This is not to say everyone should go out and befriend sex-offenders, but it forces us to ask ourselves: what are the limits of our grace? Who won't we forgive? Who won't we extend grace to? Who are the ones we consider "unclean"? Unacceptable? Unwelcome?

I'm starting to think hell is simply the place where there is no grace. Hell is where we are given labels that can never be removed, labels that define us by our darkest and dirtiest moments without any hope of change. Hell is where we allow people to stay bound up in shame afraid to come to the light for fear of being ostracized.

In contrast, heaven is where grace is freely offered before anyone has time to prove their worthiness. Heaven is where all labels are removed and prodigals are welcomed home. Heaven is the place of infinite grace. According to John's vision in Revelation, heaven is a city of grace.[7]

Life in the city has a way of testing the limits of our grace, daily. God has a way of pushing the limits of our grace until there is no one beyond our reach.

Update: Justin Tiarks

After completing the Mission Year program in 2009, Justin moved to Minnesota where he works as an administrator in a high-poverty urban charter school in the Frogtown neighborhood of St. Paul. Two-thirds of the students served by his school are immigrants and it is his goal to advocate for these beloved students and families by providing them an exceptional education and eliminating the achievement and opportunity gaps that they encounter. His Mission Year experience continues to remind him to see Jesus in the face of every student and family with whom he works.

Update: Melvin

Melvin asked Justin if he could help him move his stuff (a couple of garbage bags full of clothes) to another shelter that did welcome sex-offenders. Justin agreed. Justin met up with Melvin before moving from Chicago to Minnesota. We lost touch with Melvin until a couple years ago when one of our alums met Melvin at their church and he asked about Justin. Melvin found a church family in the city where he could be accepted and continue to grow. Please lift up a prayer for him that the grace he has received would continue to transform his life.

CHAPTER TWO

YOU DON'T KNOW $#!+:
ENCOUNTERS OF WISDOM AND HUMILITY

"Humility is the gateway into the grace and the favor of God."
- Harold Warner

"Everyone is worthy of love, except him who thinks that he is. Love is a
sacrament that should be taken kneeling."
- Oscar Wilde

We need wisdom and humility when engaging the city. The best posture with which to enter a new community is that of a learner. Being a learner offers us grace to acknowledge the leaders and wisdom already present in the communities we live and serve. By listening, learning, and confronting our own ignorance we move to mutual respect, understanding and true compassion.

You Don't Know $#!+

"He who learns must suffer. And even in our sleep, pain that cannot forget falls drop by drop upon the heart, and in our own despair, against our will, comes wisdom to us by the awful grace of God."

- Aeschylus

In my first year directing Mission Year teams in Chicago, we took our teams downtown for a homeless sleep-out to raise awareness about the needs of the homeless in order to gain empathy for what the homeless have to endure. Participants were encouraged to find cardboard and make a shelter and bed. During the event, I pulled some of our volunteers to the side and asked them if they wanted to go sleep where the homeless were actually sleeping. If trying to experience what it was like to be homeless, it made sense to do it *with* the homeless.

So we pooled our money to buy Subway sandwiches and we headed to Lower Wacker Drive, a place I knew many of the homeless sought refuge. I had passed by here many times in my car and saw the rows of clothes, blankets, and sleeping bags where many men and women found temporary shelter and escape from the brutal cold. As soon as we came up to the encampment, I approached a guy sitting on his bed. I told him we were looking to stay here for the night (I said this like I was checking into a Howard Johnson. I really had no idea what I was doing). As soon as I said this, a woman rushed over to us.

She introduced herself as "Foots," and said she was the "First Lady" of Lower Wacker Drive. She said we could stay with her, and then proceeded to lead us past where all the beds were. We walked down the street a couple hundred feet and the further we went the more concerned I became. I imagined the worst, that we were being led down some dark alley to be attacked and robbed. I tried to act cool but I was definitely on guard.

We finally turned down a small dead end side street in the bowels of Lower Wacker. Lower Wacker is a maze of winding roads underneath the city and is a popular spot for the homeless because it provides relief against the elements. Because of Foots' street cred, she had this fine piece of real estate far from the others and she was offering us shelter in her home on the street. She took a blanket and spread it out on the cold concrete and invited us to sit. We offered our Subway sandwiches but she declined.

She said, "Everyone tries to bring us food. People assume we don't have anything to eat, but we have food. What we need is money."

Then she proceeded to rummage through a big black garbage bag containing her few possessions. She gave each of us something from her bag. She gave one of us a pair of socks, another a blanket, and to one of the girls she gave a pair of shoes. We were all humbled and blown away by her generosity.

We ate our sandwiches while we talked with Foots. She told it like it was. She did not sugarcoat anything. Her words were abrasive, even cutting at times, yet there was kindness and decency in her actions. After awhile, she cut to the chase and asked us what we were doing there.

Trying to be subtle I said, "We are just looking for a place to stay for the night."

She said, "No, why are you REALLY here?" I decided to be honest since she obviously could see right through me.

"We want to spend a night on the street to better understand what it's like to be homeless." I said, bracing myself for her reaction.

At that she scoffed, "You think by sleeping outside for one night you will be able to understand what it's like? I've been homeless 27 years. You don't know what it's like to be homeless. You don't know $#!+."

I was humbled again. She was absolutely right. We didn't know jack. We couldn't possibly. But it was a start. A small opening for grace to work in us to help us better understand.

I told her "You're right, we don't know what it's like, but we want to know as much as we can." She asked us if we were "Church people." I said, "We are Christians but we are not here with a church, we are here to just be with you."

She seemed genuinely surprised that we would come with no religious agenda. After we were properly vetted, she started to open up to us. She shared how her daughter's birthday was coming up and that she regretted that she couldn't be there. She teared up from what seemed like a mixture of shame and sadness. We sat there awkwardly on the blanket trying to grasp the depths of 27 years of sorrow. She softened to us and said she was glad to have company.

At one point I had to use the bathroom and asked where I could take a leak. She pointed to a spot in the shadows a few feet away. I went over and urinated on a city street for the first time. Before that moment, I had never thought about where the homeless go to the bathroom.

Foots also told me how they are treated by cops. The cops will raid their camps and take their stuff. "My friend had his bag stolen by the police which had his social security card and ID. Now it is impossible for him to get replacements because to get a security card you have to have some form of ID, and to get ID you have to have a social security card. So now he can't get an ID or a job."

We were situated near a parking garage exit and every so often a car would come out. At one point a BMW came out and the driver just stared at us. He didn't stop. He didn't ask if we needed anything. He just stared. It seemed like we were worlds apart. We were sitting on a blanket on the sidewalk with Foots while this driver was separated by glass, heated seats, and all the luxuries he could want. The world looks different from street level. Status symbols and fancy cars just don't hold any worth compared to human bodies trying to survive on dirty city streets.

Finally, it was bedtime. We moved over to our sleeping area down the sidewalk (the opposite direction from the bathroom!). We all lay there on the unforgiving concrete trying to find a less painful position. The glowing yellow lights above us shone relentlessly throughout the night making it hard to doze off for more than 15 minutes at a time. I thought the morning would never come. I thought how lonely it must get some nights. I thought how tiring this lifestyle must be. I understood why someone might be irritable, not getting much sleep night after night, or seek something to numb the pain. When it was time to wake up, our eyes were so weary as if we had held our eyes open underwater. The stench of the street was absorbed into our clothes. Our bodies were numb and sore from the hardness of the cement.

I thought to myself, *how could Foots endure these conditions for so long?* I sensed God's Spirit leading me to ask a better question, *How could we as a society allow this to go on so long?* We didn't say much as we made our way back through the city in the morning light to our soft beds and warm homes. We had all been deeply impacted from only one night on the street. It was an experience forged into my memory. I learned an uncomfortable truth that I have never forgotten and that has served me well since: when it comes to the homeless and other groups forced to find a way to survive, I don't know shit and it's best to reserve judgment until I have spent some time in their shoes.

Update: Foots

My wife and I returned to visit Foots on her daughter's birthday to share some cake and give her some money as thanks for her kindness. She seemed tired but glad that we had remembered and came to visit. That was the last time we saw her. In an effort to remove the homeless from downtown, the city put up bars along Lower Wacker to make it harder for the homeless to seek refuge there.[1] We talked to other people who visited Lower Wacker regularly and they remembered Foots as well. She makes an impression. Even after 8 years, I think about Foots often and all the others who must do what's necessary to survive. The sacrament of that night is still working on me. I hope it will change us and challenge us to open our hearts and change our policies so that no one has to be alone and no one has to be homeless.

Cure for the White-Savior Complex

"Do you wish to rise? Begin by descending. You plan a tower that will pierce the clouds? Lay first the foundation of humility."

- St. Augustine of Hippo

I am sure you have seen movies like *Dangerous Minds*, *Freedom Writers*, or *The Blind Side*, right? You know the ones, where the white outsider comes into the "inner city" to save the poor people of color from an otherwise hopeless existence. It has been described by some as "The White-Savior Industrial Complex."[2] Hollywood loves these storylines. And so does the church.

But these kinds of stories give the false impression that people of color are just waiting for a (white) savior to come and rescue them from their situation. These movies might inspire on some level – it's great that white people are concerned and eager to help – but they give a paternalistic picture of urban communities as mere recipients. They do not show the heroic community leaders that are in every urban neighborhood, people working hard day in and day out with little resources and little recognition to improve their communities. They are leaders and mentors that we have a lot to learn from. They are the real stars that we rarely hear about.

Pat is one of those people.

I met Pat at my church and I could tell she was someone with a special heart for God and people. I decided I wanted to spend more time learning from her so I quit my job to do an internship with her and be more involved in my neighborhood. I asked my wife if she thought we could live off her salary so I could volunteer doing things in the neighborhood that were important but that I would never get paid for. My wife said we would make it work. I believe it's more important who we become than what we do, so I decided to do things that would help me become the person I wanted to be rather than simply seeking out a job that pays well. I saw something in Pat that I wanted in my life so I volunteered with her doing pastoral care at a local Christian health clinic.

While working with Pat, we visited the hospital a lot. We would go to pray with people who had been in car accidents or who had babies that were sick. Pat would tell me stories about her visits that taught me what it meant to be a pastoral presence in a person's life. She would rub patients' feet that had poor circulation and pray with them.

Pat hosted a support group for people with stress, anxiety, grief, and depression. Every Wednesday we gathered with a group of people who had experienced incredible loss. Pat, who has endured her share of grief, ran the meeting like a pastor and counselor. She spoke to their hearts and to their spirits. I was there to make coffee, pick up donuts, pass around the sign-in sheet, make people feel comfortable, and just listen. Because of Pat's experience having lost a husband and daughter, she spoke from a deep place and people trusted what she said.

Many elderly women and single moms came and shared the anxiety they had trying to make ends meet. Others opened up about horrible tragedies and loved ones lost to shootings or drugs. I started to see that poverty had an emotional as well as physical toll. As much as people needed things, they also needed comfort. They needed to be heard, cared for, and consoled. The support group was a sacrament of grace for those going through the hardest times in their life, and Pat was their priest.

After class, participants would tell Pat about a need they had and Pat would not stop until it was addressed. Whether it was finding furniture for a family whose house had just burned down or helping a single mom find a job, she was relentless. Pat is an advocate for people who have no one in their corner. We spent a lot of our time in the clinic, but my favorite times were when we went out to get a resource for someone. One time we went to deliver a wheelchair to an elderly woman who couldn't get around. Another time we picked up boxes of donated school uniforms and took them to a family of seven that had just moved to the neighborhood and had no money to purchase uniforms. On holidays, we delivered turkey baskets to elderly folks and collected funds for families that couldn't pay bills. Pat was not just meeting needs, she was bringing the good news of the kingdom. She embodied God's care, justice, and peace in ways others could tangibly feel.

Once while we were riding in the car from the hospital, I asked her how she deals with all the death, tragedy, and heavy emotional issues she faces on a daily basis. She told me about her personal practices for caring for herself, like taking hot baths after really long days. She recommended a daily devotional that she starts out her day with. I immediately picked it up and started using it. She taught me about being responsible *to* people but not being responsible *for* people. Being responsible *to* people means I help people by helping them take responsibility for their situation. Being responsible *for* people means I take their responsibility on myself which leads to burnout. This is not healthy for me or the other person. These were lessons that have proved to be invaluable to me in my ministry.

Pat is one of those remarkable people that gives a community hope. She tirelessly gives and gives with no regard for recognition or attention. She is a true inspiration. I see so many young people coming into the city wanting to start new churches and ministries right off the bat. A lot of them are very cool things, too. But sometimes I think we miss out on a powerful sacrament, not to mention a lot of wisdom, when we do not first become learners and humble ourselves under the leadership of those who are already here. It just might be the cure for the White-Savior Complex.

Being mentored by Pat and seeing the way she lives her life for others is a gift. Her life is an art of loving people and I am trying to follow her lead.

Update: Pat Herrod

Pat is a long-time North Lawndale resident and early member of Lawndale Community Church where she sings in the choir. She continues to work as a pastoral counselor at Lawndale Christian Health Clinic and serves on the boards of many community organizations. She loves her biological family deeply and has many "adopted" children.

Childlike Faith

"From childhood on I have had the dream of life lived as a sacrament... the dream implied taking life ritually as something holy."

- Bernard Berenson

I wanted to spend time with Corey* because his brother had gotten into trouble again and had been sent to the juvenile detention center just outside our neighborhood. I got free tickets to a Chicago White Sox game and invited Corey to go with me. I picked him up and he opened up about what was going on in his life. He is really smart. He just made honor roll and had above average marks. He knows his times tables and loves reading.

We had a fun time at the game. We discovered the area for kids and he was able to run, catch, throw, bat and pitch. I think it was his first time using a glove, but he picked it up quickly and had a good arm.

After the game, we were walking to the car when a homeless guy came up asking us for money. I blew him off because we did not have anything to give. Besides, I was at a game with Corey and did not want to ruin our time together. I guess I figured I had reached my quota for good deeds for the night. We walked on in silence. The all-too-familiar silence that naturally follows after you pass another human being in need and do nothing.

We walked a block or so when I heard Corey say, "I pray to God..." under his breath.

I asked, "About what?"

I thought I heard him say something about the homeless man so I asked what he said and he did not want to answer.

So I repeated my question, "You pray to God for what?"

He said, "You know."

I said, "The homeless man?"

He said, "Yes. I pray to God that he finds a place to stay and food to eat." He looked really concerned about the man when he said this and I could tell that the encounter had made an impression on him. When we got to my car, I knew he wanted to do something. I thought, "We should have gotten the quarters out of Corey's bag from the change we got at the concession stand and given them to the man." It wasn't too late.

"We could give him the quarters, the granola bar, and yogurt your mom packed. We could go find him and give it to him," I suggested, hoping to satisfy the tugging of his conscience.

He said he wanted to do it.

We drove back to where the man was. We did not see him anywhere. Corey really wanted to find him so I was praying inwardly that we would.

Then he said, "When I get older, I want to help the homeless. I want to get them a place to stay, money, and a credit card."

Then we saw the man in the middle of the street trying to get money from the cars passing by him on both sides. My heart jumped when I saw him because I really wanted to make up for my earlier response and I wanted Corey to be able to give him his gift. I rolled down my window and called him over. I explained what we had and he took it eagerly. He smiled and said, "God bless."

I told him it was all because of Corey and it put an even bigger smile on his face. We continued down the road and Corey said, "I feel good." I told him I did, too.

Then he asked if I had any church music so I put in a CD.

I felt God speaking to me through a child.

The Bible says, "Unless you change and become like little children, you will never enter the kingdom of God."[3]   Corey was showing me how to enter the kingdom of God.

It was a sweet night. It was a humbling night.

I had been schooled by a seven year old.

Update: Corey

Corey was accepted into an academically challenging high school. He will be going into his sophomore year this year. His brother is still incarcerated but is appealing his sentence. Pray for Corey to do well in his new school and for his family to experience God's peace and provision.

Rites of Passage

"In times past there were rituals of passage that conducted a boy into manhood, where other men passed along the wisdom and responsibilities that needed to be shared. But today we have no rituals. We are not conducted into manhood; we simply find ourselves there."

- Kent Nerburn

Richard Wright, an African American writer during the Harlem Renaissance, wrote intimately about the pain, anguish and complexity of black inner city youth. In the book *Rite of Passage*, Wright chronicles the downward spiral of Johnny Gibbs, a fictitious black teenager, into alienation, delinquency, and violence. He sheds light on the many factors that lead youth into gangs and anti-social behavior. He delves into the alienation, rejection, shame, and self-hatred that many youth feel. Youth turn to the streets, gangs, stealing, and mugging in order to survive and to prove themselves to others. This process, which Wright calls a "rite of passage," marks the transition for these youth away from innocence and conscience.[4] In absence of another path to manhood, this becomes the pathway for boys to feel like men. Wright seems to be urging us to interrupt this cycle. If we do not offer youth positive rites of passage into manhood, then we as a society have failed them.

I have seen many youth in our community play out this destructive cycle. Youth in the city are like all youth that go through rebellion and identity crisis in adolescence. But here the stakes are higher. Police and residents see youth as threats – public enemies – so their mistakes have graver consequences. Instead of reaching out to alienated youth with love, which is what they really need and want, society fears them and demonizes them, which only further alienates them.

The juvenile justice system is the default answer for urban youth, but it isn't working. Cook County Board President Toni Preckwinkle has been pushing to overhaul the Juvenile Detention Center. A report by the National Council on Crime and Delinquency suggested that Cook County should redirect youth to community-based alternatives to reduce the number of youth locked up. One of the striking findings from the report was that African American youths are detained *46 times the rate of white youths.*[5] According to the researchers, this is the greatest discrepancy anywhere in the country. For some youth in our neighborhood, going to prison has become a marker for how one becomes a man, but prison does not provide a healthy process of understanding life or manhood.

I think rites of passage are sorely missing and desperately needed. There is an organization in our neighborhood called Young Men's Educational Network (YMEN) who has made this their mission. They prepare young men in North Lawndale for leadership by helping them grow in their faith and character, develop a love for learning, and use their talents to serve the broader community. They commit to walk with young men through the difficult high school years and to instill in them the values and skills they need to become men. YMEN has a proven track record of educating, mentoring, and developing teenage boys into men.

Girls also need rites of passage. After studying social work at Spring Arbor University, Jaime Taylor moved to Oakland, CA in

2000 to be a part of Mission Year. She fell in love with Oakland and decided to become a permanent part of the community. Jaime saw a mentoring gap in the community so she started her own mentoring organization called Urban Mentors Network. Operating out of her house, she offers girls as well as guys, a place to come and grow into their full potential. She walks with these courageous youth through the struggles they face. She knows the youth in her neighborhood are gifted; they just need support and encouragement. She believes everyone has something to give. By mentoring youth, she has not only found her purpose, she is seeing youth discover theirs.

Mentoring offers a rite of passage for youth. A caring mentor provides a supportive structure around them. Everyone can find at least one hour a week to mentor. College students, church laypeople, retired seniors all have something to offer. We need tutors, mentors, caring adults to be involved in the lives of youth to build assets into their lives. The Search Institute conducted a study that revealed 40 developmental assets that are needed for youth to succeed.[6] Some of these assets include a young person "having three or more nonparent adults involved in their life," "having caring neighbors," being "given useful roles in community," and feeling "safe in home, school, and neighborhood." The more assets youth have in their lives, the more likely they are to engage in positive activities. The fewer assets they have, the more likely they are to engage in risky behaviors. The reason many of us did well as youth is because others built assets into our lives. The reason many youth do not do well is because they do not have enough people around them consciously and intentionally building assets into their lives. Youth from every community need people (parents, neighbors, friends, teachers, coaches, relatives, mentors) who can build assets in their lives.

Mentors can help youth stay in school and challenge them to achieve their full potential. The problem in Chicago and other neighborhoods is, too many youth are dropping out of school. The high school graduation rate in Lawndale is tragic. North Lawndale ranked 69th out of Chicago's 77 community areas with a 38.8% graduation rate in 2004 compared to a city average rate of 56.6%.[7] The public school system is broken. Jonathan Kozol, an education activist and writer, highlighted the economic disparities in educational funding in his classic book *Savage Inequalities.* In Illinois, annual funding ranges "from $2,100 on a child in the poorest district to above $10,000 in the richest. The system, 'writes John Coons, a professor of law at Berkeley University, 'bears the appearance of calculated unfairness.'"[8] More recently, 50 schools have been closed across Chicago in predominantly African American and Latino neighborhoods forcing students to travel outside their communities.[9]

Kids drop out of school for many reasons. I know youth that stop going to school because they are harassed by gangs on their way to school. Kids are passed through grades without learning what they should and then end up giving up because they don't understand what is going on. Others get recruited into selling drugs or joining gangs for protection or a sense of belonging. Many youth do not envision a future for themselves and they do not see any real connection between graduating and earning a living. One youth in my neighborhood was stressing because his grandma lost her job and said desperately, "I don't want to sell drugs, but…" The economic reality in urban communities leads to undesirable choices.

Because of all these realities, those that do persevere and go on to graduate are celebrated. In our community, graduation from elementary school and middle school are major rites of passage we celebrate. High school graduations are even bigger. Our church truly highlights education. We have a graduation Sunday where all graduates are recognized. The church seeks to create a culture where people are expected to graduate and go on to higher education.

There are schools in neighborhoods where Mission Year has served that have figured out how to raise the expectations when it comes to graduation rates. Providence St. Mel on the west side and Englewood Academy on the south side have 100% graduation rates and 100% acceptance into college.[10] They believe education is the key to breaking the cycles of poverty and they create a pathway from the cradle to college. They believe in youth and provide the right amount of challenge and support.

In our community, we celebrate every step a kid takes along the way. I was in the pastor's study of New Landmark Missionary Baptist Church, one of our church partners, on a Sunday morning when a young girl came in to show Pastor Cy Fields her progress report. She had made the honor roll and wanted him to see it. He studied it carefully and then, beaming, told her how proud he was of her. He asked if he could hold onto it and made a point to praise her accomplishments in front of the whole congregation. Every grade, subject, and level are important. Graduations are signs of progress, sacraments of celebration and achievement. They remind us, when youth are given a chance to excel they will often exceed our expectations.

Update: Jaime Taylor

Jaime has worked with youth as a support counselor for foster care youth and as a family advocate for teen mothers. She has also worked as Oakland City Director for Mission Year. Jaime began mentoring youth in her neighborhood during her Mission Year and became passionate about long-term mentoring. Twelve years later, Jaime is the founding director of the Urban Mentors Network. She is passionate about mentoring and walking alongside people the way God does…for the long haul.

Update: Pastor Cy Fields

Pastor Cy Fields is a native Chicagoan who has dedicated the past 24 years to ministry and public service. As the Senior Pastor of New Landmark Missionary Baptist Church for 10 years, Cy has seen many experience spiritual growth and develop a deeper yearning to live and give according to the mandate of Jesus. New Landmark continues to be a spiritual landmark in the East Garfield Park community and the greater Chicago metropolitan area.

CHAPTER THREE

GETTING CLEAN:
ENCOUNTERS OF BROKENNESS AND HEALING

*"It is to be broken. It is to be
torn open. It is not to be
reached and come to rest in
ever. I turn against you,
I break from you, I turn to you.
We hurt, and are hurt,
and have each other for healing.
It is healing. It is never whole."*

- Wendell Berry

Encountering the brokenness of the city helps us become more aware of our own brokenness and our need for healing. Brokenness is a gift that keeps us honest about our needs and imperfections. Because God is in all things, even our failures and brokenness can reveal God's grace to us. When we admit to what's broken, we are able to experience God's healing in the midst of our deepest pain and failure.

Getting Clean

"God, give us grace to accept with serenity the things that cannot be changed, courage to change the things which should be changed and the wisdom to distinguish the one from the other."

- Reinhold Niebuhr

Lemanuel lives on my block. He sits outside on his porch and watches everything that happens. He cares for the neighborhood and wants it to be better. He actually got onto me when we first moved in for not picking up the trash in my yard. Another time I was mowing my front yard. I thought about mowing a neighbor's front yard while I had the mower out but decided I really didn't feel like it. A couple weeks later, Lemanuel mowed all of our front yards and taught me what it really means to be a neighbor. That's the kind of guy he is.

After a year of living on our block he finally told me his story. He has been clean for 16 years. He grew up in the community. He says this is where he made his mess so he feels responsible now to clean it up and make it better. So for the last 16 years he has been involved with AA and leading meetings for other guys in the community that have not yet kicked the habit. He believes the Bible and the 12 Steps are a powerful combination. His trademark expression is "God first!" which he shouts out to people he knows as they go by. He credits God for his recovery and is grateful to God for being clean for so long.

Mark* is someone I see around the neighborhood too. I met Mark when he was part of our church's recovery ministry for men struggling to overcome drug and alcohol addiction. He was thriving in the program but then Mark relapsed. He started hanging out with old friends and returning to old habits. When I saw him on the street afterwards, I hardly recognized him. His face was drained of life and his eyes were glazed. It's been four years since he relapsed and he is still caught in the snare of drug addiction. Every time I see him, I am grieved by and reminded of the hopelessness and cycles of addiction that many men and women face on the streets. It is heartbreaking.

That is why Lemanuel does what he does. He has planted himself in his old neighborhood to pull out as many guys as he can in the time he has left. Whenever I have someone new over to our house and Lemanuel is around he will say, "Tell them my story." So I recite the story. It's a ritual for us now. It is a reminder, when it is so easy to be overwhelmed by despair, that change is possible. He is a visible witness of an invisible power. So Lemanuel sits boldly on his front porch for all to see, a testimony of healing and hope for those like me who need reminders.

Update: Lemanuel

This year will make 18 years of sobriety for Lemanuel. He continues to lead guys through "the steps" of Alcoholics Anonymous and is a requested speaker for many recovery programs. Lemanuel continues to sit on his porch and remind the community to put "God first."

Update: Mark

Mark has gotten clean. He was recently married and is looking for a job. Please pray for him as he rebuilds and tries to stay clean.

Cracks

"There's a crack, a crack in everything. That's how the light gets in. That's how the light gets in."

- Leonard Cohen

Dave Clark, a veteran urban minister in Chicago who works for the Christian Community Development Association (CCDA), once told a new crop of Mission Year volunteers that God will shine a light on all the cracks in our life while we are serving in the city. This is so true. God has a way of using the city to reveal our damaged walls. Some people come to the city to avoid issues or to run away from problems back home. When God shines light on the cracks, it takes people by surprise. We have had some people leave the city because it was too hard to deal with their own cracks, much less anyone else's. Sometimes we want to focus on other people and their needs so we don't have to address our own. Sometimes we want to look good on the outside so we cover up the cracks. But the cracks are where God wants to work.

Cornel West says, "We are all cracked vessels trying to love our crooked neighbors with our crooked hearts." I am reminded of this daily as politicians, pastors, and prophets publically confess their personal and professional failures. I am reminded when I look out my window and see drug dealers, addicts, and ex-offenders playing out destructive patterns. Most importantly, I am reminded every day when I see the cracks in my own crooked heart: anger, impatience, bitterness, jealousy, greed, lust, selfishness, vanity... the list goes on. It is easy to think pretty highly of ourselves as we look at all the things that are messed up in the world, but the truly enlightened person understands that the seeds of all the evil in the world are within each of us.

Thomas Merton understood this as well as anyone: "Instead of hating the people you think are war-makers, hate appetites and disorder in your own soul, which are the causes of war. If you love peace, then hate injustice, hate tyranny, hate greed—but hate these things in yourself, not in another."[1]

When we examine ourselves, we cannot hide from the fact that we all are cracked. But the amazing thing is that God is revealed in cracked vessels. Corinthians says, "we have this treasure in earthen vessels so that the surpassing greatness of the power will be of God and not of ourselves."[2] Our cracks are where God's power shows up. I have experienced this when sharing my own testimony with others. The places where I have experienced the deepest pain and shame have often been the places that God has gotten the greatest glory. Do not be afraid to let God shine a light on the cracks in your life.

A place of divine encounter and transformation that helps us face pain from the past is counseling. I am a big fan of counseling. I have seen God work in the context of counseling in profound ways. When we deal with the past, we can find greater freedom and healing. God can only heal what is brought to light. When we hide or bury our hurts we cannot be healed and move forward.

I recommend counseling to many people who move to the city. They come to the city to serve but the city ends up showing them that they are just as broken as the city and in need of healing. This is a gift of grace, yet we don't always experience it as such.

People often fight the idea of counseling at first. There is a stigma that counseling is only for people with severe mental issues. This is a lie that keeps people from receiving healing. If our arm was severed, we would go to the hospital. We wouldn't think twice. When we are emotionally severed, we need to go to counseling.

I've seen hardened men going through recovery break down in a group counseling session as they open up about repressed memories from childhood. They don't realize how the guilt and shame buried deep inside them is at the root of their addiction to alcohol and drugs. I've also seen suburban women finally begin to acknowledge and deal with the repercussions of family abuse. The counseling setting provides a safe place for people to open up and allow the Holy Spirit to work in our lives.

The Holy Spirit is the "Counselor."[3] I have experienced the Holy Spirit most noticeably in my life in the counseling context. Jesus said the Spirit will "guide you into all the truth."[4] Counseling allows us to speak the truth of our experiences and the truth truly "sets us free."[5] The grace the city gives us is the recognition and acceptance of our brokenness. If we don't acknowledge it, we remain stuck, captives to the past. By addressing our brokenness, we see that God longs for our healing and leads us through our brokenness to truth and wholeness.

By admitting our brokenness, it puts us on a level footing with those we come to serve. We are not perfect people helping needy people. We are broken people working alongside other broken people. As Henri Nouwen puts it, we are "wounded healers."

I had a conversation with a Christian brother who had made a serious lapse in judgment. He felt very beat up. He had felt a call to ministry but after making a major slipup he wasn't sure if God could still use him. We talked about righteousness and integrity and how important that is for those going into the ministry. I then shared with him how many of the saints and prophets that we admire and imitate today have made some pretty epic mistakes. His eyes lit up with hope that maybe it was still possible that God could use him.

Of course it is. That's all God has to work with. God loves healing cracked vessels and using them to display the power and beauty of God. We are all cracked vessels, but we are loved. And if we allow God to shine light on our cracks, then God can still use us for great things.

Ashleigh Hill, a poet and Mission Year alumna in Chicago, wrote this poem after hearing stories of survival from teen moms at the transitional shelter where she worked. It speaks of our cracked yet beautiful lives:

Song #1

I have a blue song in my heart.

I have a blue, red, black, white, yellow, orange, brown song

in my heart.

I have a song in my heart

fracturing apart

down through my finger tips

and cold toes,

I have a song in my heart

and captives
and bottles
shoved deep into the coat pockets
and basements
of my deep, dark heart.
I have a cracked song in my cracked heart.

I have a beautiful song in my heart,
all broken and whole like Christ
in my heart.

Some days,
I have a weak song in my heart.
I have a picked over and purpled song
in my bruised heart.

Still,
I have a free song in my heart,
full of bells going off,
ringing up to my ears
and fixed temple.
I have a song in my heart
and stories
and truth
invading like the uncut roots
and redundant weeds

of my deep, dark heart.

I have a mended song in my mended heart.

I have a beautiful song in my heart,

all broken and whole like Christ

in my heart.

And I wake up every day praying for people

to sing the lyrics with me.

Update: Ashleigh Hill

After growing up on the east coast, Ashleigh moved to Chicago to do Mission Year in 2009. She has worked in the city with women, teenagers, and LGBTQ youth experiencing homelessness. Ashleigh is a poet and runs A Fractured Life project, which offers resources for Christians seeking to understand the connections between gender, sexuality, race, violence, poverty, and faith. She is currently the Development Coordinator for Mission Year.

ER

"If you conceal your disease, you cannot expect to be cured."
- Ethiopian Proverb

Having been involved in pastoral care in the city, I have had regular visits to the emergency room. Sitting in a waiting room in the city is a unique experience. Rarely do you get such an intimate view of the suffering and pain of a city in one room. It is a collection of all the traumas and tragedies that one day holds for some of the most vulnerable people in the city.

To sit there is a reminder of our common humanity. We all bleed, puke, and get diarrhea. Money can get us better service and care and help prevent some illnesses, but it cannot completely keep us from car accidents or common colds. We all find ourselves at one point or another in the ER. And I don't know why, but somehow it always seems to be around 1 a.m. In that moment, we share a common experience with the other worried friends and family that have also raced to the hospital to care for their loved ones.

I remember one trip to the ER very well. I went with one of our Mission Year volunteers who was having severe stomach pains in the middle of the night. We walked into the ER and they quickly gave us a bed while we waited to see the doctor. Two other people came in while we were waiting. The first was an elderly African American man and the second was a young white teenager.

The doctors assumed the older man was homeless because of how he looked and they refused him treatment. He started to foam at the mouth and have convulsions right next to us. We looked on with wide eyes, wondering if we were about to see someone die in front of us. We started praying under our breath. After it became obvious the man had a legitimate condition, they finally went over and started taking care of him.

The young white teenager who came in around the same time had a spiked Mohawk and was dressed in black. A policeman brought him in and sat him down in a wheelchair to rest. We heard him say he had consumed too much alcohol and just needed to sleep it off. When the doctors came to see our volunteer, they assumed he was with the young man and was there for similar reasons. Ironically, our volunteer was serving with a homeless shelter for the year and probably had more in common with the elderly African American man than the wasted white kid.

All around us judgments and assumptions were being made. Judgments based on how someone dressed, what color their skin was, or how old they were. I caught myself making judgments too. When the police officer dropped off the young white kid who had been caught partying hard, my immediate thought was, I bet he wouldn't do the same thing if the kid had been black. I made a judgment about the cop and I knew nothing about him. So often we make snap judgments of people. We pretend to know who they are before we have any opportunity to get to know them. Even doctors in the ER who are supposedly guided by scientific methods are influenced and affected by their cultural bias.

Pre-judging people can keep some from being treated (literally) like human beings. Whether or not a person is homeless should not determine what kind of treatment they receive from the hospital. And just because a cop is helping a white kid tonight does not mean he would not do the same for a black kid. I simply cannot know that. To judge someone in an instant is unfair. Prejudice is a disease that, if left undiagnosed, can destroy our being. Luckily, the city has a way of surfacing the sickness.

The ER is a place of quick decisions, snap judgments, and crisis. It is a place where we can get a glimpse of our common struggles and humanity. It is also a place that reflects the brokenness of the world. Not only our physical sicknesses and infirmities, but also our inward sickness and prejudice. The ER is evidence we are all in need of healing.

Epic Failures

"Life is a series of failures punctuated by a few brief successes."

- James Altucher

I have a confession. I am not a big fan of Christian conferences. In fact, I sometimes get nauseous listening to the outrageous success stories coming from the main stages. Not because I don't appreciate hearing the good things God is doing, I do. It's just that I know it's not the whole story.

I know people need to be motivated to serve (and give). I know hearing positive stories helps us all believe change is possible. But sometimes I would like to hear a good failure story. I can relate more with that. I think it's dishonest when we share the successes without showing the other side. I actually think we miss out on something profound when we omit the failures. If God is in all things, then that means God is just as present in our failures as in the successes.

I recently discovered a new truth in a familiar parable. It's the parable of the sower, the story about the seed that falls on four different types of soil.[6] In the parable, the sower scatters the seed all over, but only one of the four soils ends up being good soil. Wait, did you catch that? Only one fourth of the sower's efforts produced anything. That means three-fourths of the sower's efforts failed!

If this parable is indicative of our ministry then we should expect three-fourths of our efforts to utterly fail. It should actually be more surprising if it doesn't fail! This is very freeing to me. This should give all of us hope when things don't turn out how we want or hope.

But there's more to the story. Jesus says that one-fourth will produce a harvest 30, 60, even 100 times that which was sown. This means, you will fail more often than not, but what does come from your efforts is completely worth it. You may not reach a whole neighborhood or city, but that handful of relationships you pour into will in turn impact other relationships which will impact other relationships and so on. Church attendance and counting conversions may not be the best signs of ministry impact. Perhaps it's the moments of human connection, the relationships where roots go deep, life is truly shared, and mutual investments made that count most.

Failure is not something to fear or hide. The gospels are full of stories of failure. The disciples are failing at everything: fighting for power, falling asleep in prayer, unable to drive out demons, fleeing the scene during Jesus' most critical moment, missing the point of Jesus' stories and actions, preventing children from getting to Jesus, and selling Jesus out for money. The failures do not take away from the gospel's power. The gospel of grace is actually revealed through their failures. The gospels we read are stories of how God uses failure to bring about redemption in the world. God can do the same through our stories!

So I like sharing stories of failure. Paul said he boasts in his weakness so that God's power may be revealed.[7] I have found God in my own failure. In my efforts at holiness I kept falling short. I thought God expected perfection from me so I lived in constant shame. Then I had mentors that really helped me understand grace. God loved me and chose to die for me when I was at my deepest and darkest point. I don't have to earn God's love, I'm already loved. Accepting that grace was actually what allowed me to find victory in areas of my life that for years I had failed.

In *Tattoos on the Heart*, Gregory Boyle says, "Anything worth doing is worth failing at." Whether it's ministry, marriage, mentoring, leadership, discipleship or missionary service, if it is worth doing, then it is worth failing at. Maybe you failed in the past and thought God can't use you. Or you are such a perfectionist you live in constant fear of failing so you never even attempt anything great. Maybe you have experienced too much defeat you have given up trying. It's time to embrace failure as the grace it is.

I have experienced some big failures since being in Chicago. One project I worked on very hard completely collapsed. I spent two years working on it before realizing it was not going to happen. I made several mistakes along the way. I realized that I was operating way outside my gifts. I stepped into a role I didn't feel comfortable being in, doing things for which I did not have the knowledge or expertise. I had gotten in over my head, and had taken on more than I had the resources and support to do well. I also did not listen to my own concerns about tackling such a big project. I had to learn the hard way.

Failure has taught me my worth is not in my performance or achievements. Giving myself freedom to fail has helped me give grace to others. When we are so afraid of failing, we get paralyzed and can't do anything. When we fear failure, we stop taking risks. I realized God lets us fail. God doesn't care about our egos. God doesn't care about building our reputations or personal kingdoms. But I've also learned God doesn't waste any of our experiences. When we submit our failures, God can use our inevitable miscalculations and poor decisions. I may not have succeeded in what I set out to do, but I did establish critical relationships, learned valuable skills, realized what I'm not good at, supported the vision of community leaders, and let the community know I was there with them in the struggle even when things didn't go like we wanted. My scars and disappointment deepened my commitment to be an agent of change in the city.

Ultimately, we are not judged by results. We are not a better person if we succeed or a lesser person if we fail. Failure can lead us to where true significance and meaning lies. Thomas Merton said it well:

"Do not depend on the hope of results. You may have to face the fact that your work will be apparently worthless and even achieve no results at all, if not perhaps results opposite to what you expect. As you get used to this idea, you start more and more to concentrate not on the results, but on the value, the rightness, the truth of the work itself. You gradually struggle less and less for an idea and more for specific people. In the end, it is the reality of personal relationships that saves everything."

CHAPTER FOUR

BEST VACATION EVER:
ENCOUNTERS OF REMEMBRANCE AND REST

"What you remember saves you."
- W. S. Merwin

"I've given my life to the principle and the ideal of memory, and remembrance."
- Elie Wiesel

Remembrance and rest are crucial in sustaining ourselves in the city. Remembering helps us discover grace in forgotten and unlikely places and teaches us to pay more attention to God, ourselves and others. Sabbath rest is a grace with the power to liberate us from the demands of doing good. As we rest, we acknowledge our human limitations and we remember God is able. Remembrance not only brings us into communion with God, it brings us into solidarity with those who suffer.

Best Vacation Ever

"What we have once enjoyed we can never lose. All that we love deeply becomes a part of us."

- Helen Keller

In an attempt to get the kids talking, Mary Cray, a retired public school teacher who volunteers as a tutor with Celestial Ministries, went around the room asking students random questions. Every Saturday morning, youth from the west side of Chicago are provided a safe place to reflect, create, and express themselves through music and dance. Started as a ministry of support for children and families with incarcerated loved ones, Celestial Ministries has become a secondary family for many in the North Lawndale community.

Tyrese*, a seven-year-old student in our junior drumline, was asked, "What was your best vacation and what made it so good?" As he paused to speak, I became very curious as to what he might say. I thought back to family vacations I had experienced growing up. We would take family trips during the summer to places like the Smoky Mountains in North Carolina or to see the monuments in Washington D.C. I wondered if Tyrese had ever been outside of the State of Illinois, or Chicago for that matter.

My internal quandary was interrupted when Tyrese shouted out, "When I visited my dad in prison, because I have fun with my dad!"

After Tyrese spoke, there was a brief moment of sacred silence in the room. For me, it was a reminder of why we do what we do. Amidst frantic drum practices and tough teen facades, there is pain and loneliness. And regardless of the guilt or innocence of those incarcerated, it is the innocent children and families that are forced to pay the heaviest price. It is not right or just that Tyrese's best vacation is visiting a prison.

The truth is, the prison system is a destructive and violent force in the lives of children and families in our community. One study showed that over 57% of our neighborhood is involved in the prison system in some way – either in prison, on parole, or on probation.[1] That means the majority of kids and youth in our community have loved ones who are incarcerated.

In *The New Jim Crow: Mass Incarceration in the Age of Colorblindness,* Michelle Alexander shines a light on the injustice in our prison system. The United States has more people incarcerated than any other nation (2.2 million), almost half of which are African American. She reports there are more black men incarcerated now than were enslaved in 1850. Blacks and Latinos are incarcerated at disproportionate rates even though research shows that whites, blacks, and Latinos commit crimes around the same rate. Alexander argues that the mass incarceration of low-income minorities is causing the same discriminatory effects in areas of housing, education, voting, and employment as Jim Crow laws did, and as a result is creating a permanent under-class.[2] When you lock up that many fathers (and mothers) you aren't just punishing the parents, you are hurting the children.

What do we do as Christians when confronted with these harsh realities? The Bible urges us to "remember those in prison, as if you were together with them in prison."[3] Jesus knew what it was like to have a loved one incarcerated. His cousin, John the Baptist, was falsely accused and arrested (and executed). Jesus identified so strongly with those in prison, he told his disciples when they visit the prisoner, they are visiting him.[4] As a victim of false imprisonment and injustice, Jesus must have also understood how prisons are used in Empires to serve the interests of the powerful. Just survey prisons in the Bible and you will see they are used over and over as means of exploitation and injustice. I have hope though, because Jesus came "to set prisoners free."[5] That is how I know that Jesus is on Tyrese's side.

As many of us will enjoy a spring break, summer or Christmas vacation with family this year, let us remember those in prison and the children and families that are serving time without them. I hope you will not only give presents through programs like Angel Tree,[6] I hope you will think about volunteering and supporting organizations working year-round to support families. And as you get to know those children and families, I also hope you will be compelled to advocate for just policies that will set prisoners like Tyrese's dad free.[7]

Update: Tyrese

Tyrese is now 12 years old and in the sixth grade. He loves basketball and is being coached by a professional basketball player from the North Lawndale community. His father is still incarcerated. Please pray that Tyrese and his family experience God's abundant life.

Update: Mary Cray

Mary marched with Dr. King during the Civil Rights movement and went on to spend 20 years teaching in North Lawndale. Now, she is focused on environmental issues and serves as Director of Save the Prairie Society where she brings groups from the city to the prairie. She believes there's something about the outdoors that speaks to and inspires people.

Sabbath Keeping

"Work is not always required. There is such a thing as sacred idleness."
- *Gordon MacDonald*

I have a hard time taking Sabbath. Sometimes I feel like seven days is not enough time to do all that needs to be done. How in the world could I take a Sabbath? But I'm starting to discover how important taking Sabbath is. Sabbath helps me remember that the world will go on without me. The world is not on my shoulders. The stress and pressure I feel, like everything depends on me, is false.

Sabbath is liberation. Taking Sabbath helps free me from the demands others place on me and the demands I place on myself. Thomas Merton warned about the dangers of doing good:

"There is a pervasive form of contemporary violence to which the idealist fighting for peace by nonviolent means most easily succumbs: activism and overwork. The rush and pressure of modern life are a form, perhaps the most common form, of its innate violence. To allow oneself to be carried away by a multitude of conflicting concerns, to surrender to too many projects, to want to help everyone in everything is to succumb to violence....The frenzy of the activist neutralizes his work for peace. It destroys his own inner capacity for peace. It destroys the fruitfulness of his own work, because it kills the root of inner wisdom which makes work fruitful."[8]

Sabbath protects us from the voices within that tell us we are never doing enough. Our work can become an idol, whether it's ministry or marketing, bible study or banking. It is so easy to find our worth and significance in what we do rather than in God and who we are. Prophetic theologian Walter Breuggeman says, "Sabbath breaks the vicious cycle of production and consumerism." By remembering the Sabbath we are remembering that we are sacred beings made to create and not just consume. We have divine permission to rest, create, and pursue the things that bring us life.

Sabbath helps us care for ourselves. Remembering the Sabbath allows us to slow down and stop defining ourselves by what we do. We remember God is not the one demanding our endless work. Sabbath is actually an act of faith. By keeping the Sabbath, God is offering us an invitation to rest and find that God is enough. Sabbath requires us to trust that God is able to handle our burdens and the burdens of the world.

Sabbath is grace. Sandy Henkel, from Here's Life Inner City in Roseland, once spoke to our Mission Year teams about the importance of Sabbath for sustaining ourselves in ministry. Sandy has been living in Roseland for 19 years. Sandy told us, "Sabbath is a gift from God. We do not receive it to our detriment." Through Sabbath God is offering us spiritual and physical rest, renewal, and restoration. After sharing all the joys and benefits of Sabbath she asked us rhetorically, "Why would we not accept such a precious gift?" It's a good question. Most likely, it is not because we don't want or need a Sabbath, it's that we don't make time for it.

We build a Sabbath day into our Mission Year lifestyle so our volunteers can have a day to recharge and sustain themselves over the long haul. We encourage them to do the things that bring them life. I often hear from our participants that taking a Sabbath is one of the most impactful parts of their year of service and it is one of the things they want to continue doing after their Mission Year.

One of the things I love to do on my Sabbath is go to a local park. Almost every city has a park. Chicago is so filled with parks the official motto of the city is "Urbs in horto," which is Latin for, "City in a Garden."[9] No matter what neighborhood in Chicago you live in, chances are you can find a park close by. Douglas Park, our closest park, is about a mile away from our house. Once the Spring comes we go there regularly to enjoy nature or have some recreation.

The parks are great because they are free and open to everyone. They are some of the few places where so many different people intersect in the city. Chicago is very segregated. But the parks with their soccer fields and basketball courts, track, fishing ponds, field houses and beautiful landscaping bring people from all backgrounds and neighborhoods together. The parks stand in contrast to the rest of the city that is divided by race, economics, and status.

Henri Nouwen said, "The whole of nature is a sacrament pointing to a reality far beyond itself." In Revelation, there is a picture of a City in a Garden.[10] It is Jerusalem, the city of God. It is an image of the divine and human coming together in unity (where the visible reality and the invisible grace merge into one). Parks point us to the great city in a garden where all barriers are broken down and we experience the redemption of the city. We will enjoy the best of heaven and earth in one place. We will experience our wholeness along with the wholeness of the entire created world. Sabbath reminds us of and connects us into God's desire for the renewal of the whole world.

Maybe you have felt too busy for a Sabbath or maybe you haven't really taken the invitation seriously enough. I think sometimes we forget Sabbath is one of the Ten Commandments right up there with, "Thou shall not kill." And rightly so, because remembering the Sabbath for us workaholics and activists, may end up being an issue of life and death. Sabbath preserves our lives and our ability to sustain ourselves in the work we do in the city. The prayer of Oscar Romero is one of my life prayers that highlights the need to step back and recognize our own limitations.[11] It reminds me that I am just a small part of the bigger movement of God. I pray that we will find liberation from our addiction to doing so we can become free to be the people God is calling us to be.

It helps, now and then, to step back and take a long view.
The kingdom is not only beyond our efforts, it is even beyond our vision.
We accomplish in our lifetime only a tiny fraction
of the magnificent enterprise that is God's work.
Nothing we do is complete, which is a way of saying
that the kingdom always lies beyond us.
No statement says all that could be said.
No prayer fully expresses our faith.
No confession brings perfection.

No pastoral visit brings wholeness.

No program accomplishes the church's mission.

No set of goals and objectives includes everything.

It may be incomplete,

but it is a beginning, a step along the way,

an opportunity for the Lord's grace to enter and do the rest.

We may never see the end results, but that is the difference

between the master builder and the worker.

We are workers, not master builders; ministers, not messiahs.

We are prophets of a future not our own.

This is what we are about.

We plant the seeds that one day will grow.

We water seeds already planted,

knowing that they hold future promise.

We lay foundations that will need further development.

We provide yeast that produces far beyond our capabilities.

We cannot do everything, and there is a sense of liberation

in realizing that. This enables us to do something,

and to do it very well. Amen.

Interruptions

"The great thing, if one can, is to stop regarding all the unpleasant things as interruptions of one's 'own,' or 'real' life. The truth is of course that what one calls the interruptions are precisely one's real life -- the life God is sending one day by day."

- C. S. Lewis

The city has helped me learn how God can be encountered in daily interruptions.

One Friday, I was meeting with a Mission Year volunteer at a McDonald's downtown when an energetic man came over to our table and started talking to us. He shared his story about how he had gone from a well-paying job to being homeless to being an up and coming street magician. He told us about his passion for magic which went back to childhood and showed us some impressive card tricks. He was very open about the setbacks he had experienced in life and despite being noticeably tired due to lack of sleep, he had a contagious hope about his future. We listened for awhile but then broke off the conversation because we had somewhere else to be.

The following Sunday, a group of Mission Year alumni met up at a coffeeshop to discuss a book we have been reading together. After a few minutes of discussion, we were interrupted by a guy sitting next to us who was working on his computer. He couldn't help but hear us talking about Christians and was curious to know about the book we were reading. We told him the name of the book and gave him a synopsis. He was a Christian and he shared a little about himself. At this point he began asking us unrelated questions and I was afraid this would detract from our conversation. As politely

91

as I could I told him we didn't have a lot of time to discuss the book and that we needed to get back to our discussion.

The next day, I was in Roseland for a monthly check-in with a volunteer. We walked over to a Wendy's near his work site and found a table where we could talk. As he was sharing about what had been going on for him lately, a guy ventured over to us and sat down at the table right next to us. I saw him coming and braced myself for yet another interruption. He said he can tell we were Christians (did he hear our conversation or is that just a good panhandler opening line?). He began to tell us his story which included an experience he had with God telling him to take care of his mom who lives down the street. He also told us he had some mental illness and showed us his medication to prove it. We sat there listening and at the end he asked us if we could help him out with anything. We didn't have any money so he moved on and we went back to our conversation.

Three days. Three interruptions. These encounters remind me of something Henri Nouwen said, "My whole life I have been complaining that my work was constantly interrupted, until I discovered the interruptions were my work." I am realizing my work involves listening, discerning, and reflecting on the interruptions as much as the scheduled moments.

Interruptions have a way of revealing things we would not know otherwise. Like a pop-quiz, interruptions test our motives, our assumptions, and our priorities. Sometimes we pass, sometimes we fail. Sometimes it is not so clear.

In each situation above, we did practice a ministry of presence, we acknowledged the person's existence and listened with sensitivity and care. On the other hand, in each situation, time hindered the length of our encounters as well as tested our patience with each individual. Each interruption took up precious time which required us to navigate our way out of the conversation. Malcolm Gladwell, in *The Tipping Point*, writes about a study done at Princeton Seminary that tested the factors most important in determining if a seminarian would respond to someone in need.[12] Some seminarians were asked to prepare a sermon on the Good Samaritan while others were asked to talk about the relevance of clergy to the religious vocation. They were also given surveys to gauge their levels of compassion. On their way to make the presentation, some students were told they were late and better get moving, while others were told they had a few minutes but they could go ahead over. Along the way, each student ran into a man slumped in an alley who was coughing and groaning. What they found was that it didn't matter if they were preaching on the Good Samaritan or if they were highly compassionate people in general, the only thing that really mattered was whether the student was in a rush. The perception of being late had the effect of turning someone who was ordinarily compassionate into someone who was indifferent to suffering. Like the study, I discovered I can be stingy with my time and neglect opportunities for compassion, or at least cut my compassion short.

I know I am not obligated to help everyone; it is not only impossible, it can be unhealthy. Sometimes we need to cut short the conversation and other times we need to sit in the awkwardness to see what God may be doing. This is where discernment is needed. Discernment is a messy process because it involves making judgments in the moment (does this person just want money?, Is this guy going to be a distraction?, is this person trying to manipulate me with his story?).

Sometimes our judgments are right and sometimes we are proven very wrong. As I think on these encounters I am reminded how badly people need human contact. Each person wanted, maybe even needed, to tell their story, be heard, acknowledged by another human being. Each person was outside community wanting to be included in the circle. Isn't that what every one of us desires?

And didn't each of those people reflect the divine in a way that could benefit our community? The street magician had a passion for what he did and a hope for the future despite his present circumstances. The café Christian had a boldness to risk rejection and reach out to a group of fellow Christians. The Wendy's witness showed me that sometimes obediently following God's call requires us to ask others for help.

Did I pass or fail? I don't know. But I know those moments have allowed me to remember that the interruptions are part of my work, that time is not more important than people, that each person reflects the divine in ways I can benefit, and that hopefully with each interruption I will learn to respond a little bit more like the one I claim to follow.

CHAPTER FIVE

VIOLENCE INTERRUPTERS:
ENCOUNTERS OF PEACE AND RECONCILIATION

"To not work for reconciliation is to be in rebellion against God."
- John Perkins

"I take literally the statement in the Gospel of John that God loves the world. I believe that the world was created and approved by love, that it subsists, coheres, and endures by love, and that, insofar as it is redeemable, it can be redeemed only by love. I believe that divine love, incarnate and indwelling in the world, summons the world always toward wholeness, which ultimately is reconciliation and atonement with God."
- Wendell Berry

The heart of the gospel is reconciliation. We are called to be agents of reconciliation and peace in the midst of division and conflict. Communion is more than grace for personal sin, it's grace to heal the divides and violence we inflict on each other. Peace and reconciliation take crossing borders and building bridges. Peace may be our most credible witness in the world.

Violence Interrupters

"Are peacemakers prepared to take the same risks in making peace that soldiers are prepared to take in making war?"

- Daniel Berrigan

I am tired of the violence I see in the world. Senseless violence. Tragic loss. Agonizing grief. How do we cope with the acts of violence we have seen across our country in places like Colorado, Portland, and Connecticut? Troubling trends in youth violence. Communities shocked and shattered by destruction. Precious young lives taken prematurely and undeservedly. This is not how it should be.

Yet, this unimaginable tragedy is an all-too-familiar reality in neighborhoods in Chicago. In 2012 alone, there were 500 homicides in Chicago.[1] I went to a vigil where they read the name of every child whose life had been taken in the last three years. Hearing the names of hundreds of children and youth read aloud was enough to make me want to shout out, "Enough!" How many more names do we have to read before we are moved to action?

I've marched for peace in the streets with neighbors, community groups, concerned churches, and family members who have lost their loved ones to gun violence. Our Mission Year teams attend funerals and grieve alongside communities who experience this personal trauma on a weekly basis. Two years ago, 6 year old Aliyah Shell, was shot by a stray bullet while playing on her front porch. There was a huge community rally following her death and Pastor Victor Rodriguez, one of our church partners, passionately pled for the violence to stop. He called on the churches to get outside the walls of the church. He even asked for forgiveness from the gang members that Christians had not worked harder to connect with them.

We have a lot to learn from communities who endure this kind of sorrow and death daily. They have to find ways to remember lives lost and keep hope in the midst of agonizing loss. Communities find ways to memorialize the youth so that they remain names and faces rather than just cold statistics. T-shirts are made and worn in remembrance, street shrines of candles, signs, and stuffed animals are set up, tattoos with names and faces are imprinted, peace marches organized, and political action taken to not let their memories fade with the media cycle.

The day after the Newtown tragedy in Connecticut I drove through the city and I saw flags at half mast outside all the public schools I passed. I was touched by the solidarity. Our city understands sorrow and suffering and we stand with others who are experiencing it. I hope this marks a larger solidarity. That when children and youth in Chicago and other parts of the country and world suffer, those in Connecticut, Portland, and Colorado will stand with us.

I hope we can connect the violent dots. All life is precious. Whether it's happening in suburban Colorado or inner city Chicago, Portland or Palestine, Connecticut or Calcutta. Amy Williams, an urban youth worker who specializes in gang-affiliated youth, says "all youth are at-risk youth." She calls herself a hope dealer and seeks to bring hope to youth who are trapped in destructive cycles of violence. Amy's right, all youth need support, love, mentoring, guidance and opportunities. A recent study by the University of Chicago Crime Lab in partnership with Chicago Public Schools shows that mentoring and counseling dramatically decreases violence among high-risk students.[2] Yet youth programs, social services, and guidance counselors are constantly being cut from our schools and communities. The violence in the city and in other places in our world is telling us that our youth are hurting, suffering with alienation, anger, depression, and a host of mental disorders. We can't pretend this is an isolated incident. It's systemic.

Jean Vanier said, "I believe every act of violence is also a message that needs to be understood. Violence should not be answered just by greater violence but by real understanding. We must ask: 'Where is the violence coming from? What is its meaning?'" If there is a message in the violence for us I believe it is this: we are one human family and every one of our lives matters. Every child counts and deserves to experience abundant life. We need to invest in our youth. Investing in youth saves lives. In the city, many churches can't afford to hire youth pastors. Many urban youth workers do it on a volunteer basis. Many community organizations are reaching out to youth out of their homes operating on shoestring budgets. All this while gun lobbyists are spending billions to convince our political representatives to ease up on gun restrictions. Every one of us needs to be a lobbyist for children and youth in this country.

The documentary *The Interrupters*, came out in 2013 highlighting the work of CeaseFire, a gang violence intervention organization here in Chicago. They call themselves violence interrupters because they purposefully go into high-conflict situations to keep things from escalating into violence. To work for peace means we have to enter into the violence. Daniel Berringan, a Jesuit priest who spoke out against the Vietnam War in the 60's asked, "Are peacemakers prepared to take the same risks to make peace as soldiers are prepared to take to make war?"

Jesus said, "Blessed are the peacemakers, for they will be called children of God."[3] Jesus entered into the violence. The cross that we see every Sunday in church should remind us of our radical call to witness to peace in a violent world. Most of us like the idea of peace but we don't want to have anything to do with violence. But the reality of violence gives us the opportunity and responsibility to embrace our unique call to peacemaking.

One of my friends has made peacemaking part of her vocation. Tiffany Childress-Price is a committed Christian and teacher at North Lawndale College Prep in the neighborhood where I live. She is also a certified trainer in Kingian nonviolence. She takes King's principles of nonviolence and teaches them at her school so youth are empowered with alternative ways of dealing with their problems. "Our particular practice is called Kingian Nonviolence and out of that we have peer jury, peer mediation, peace circles," Tiffany said in an interview with ABC News about her work.[4] Tiffany suggested a structure for creating and keeping peace after noting a spike in violence about five years ago. She began the model by recruiting "peace warriors" within the school to be on the lookout for conflict. "As we have a metric for academic achievement, we wanted to have a metric for peace. We set the goal for 90 percent, an A-minus, and we measure that by the number of days out of 170 school days out of which we've had no violence. So every year we've hit that," said Childress-Price.

"To be a peace warrior is basically to be a nomad for peace. You know how to facilitate peace if it's broken and how to keep it and maintain it," said Ladavia Bennett, one of the school's peace warriors. "We try our hardest to keep down tension in school, in the hallways, classrooms, around the school period and me personally, I try to do it when I'm outside of school, in everyday life," said Kimberly Stuart, another peace warrior.

Students are now finding creative ways to work for peace in their school and community. While many in our city are decrying the violence among youth in the city, Tiffany is creating a culture of nonviolence and peace in the place where she lives and works.

Christ came to bring peace to the world. This peace is not the avoidance of conflict or violence. Peace enters into the violence and seeks to understand, mediate, and advocate in the midst of the madness.

What if we all became violence interrupters? What if we all looked for ways to increase peace in our everyday lives, communities, and cities? Jesus came to teach us the way of peace. Peace may be our most credible witness to the world.

Update: Tiffany Childress-Price

Tiffany has been studying Kingian Nonviolence directly with Dr. Bernard Lafayette (Poor People's Campaign Director of 1968 and colleague of Dr. King) and other nonviolent practitioners over the last 5 years. After bringing the training to her school she has seen transformation on a number of levels. Her work, led by students, has been documented on *ABC News, Rethinking Schools, Facing History and Ourselves,* and *NPR.* Despite the progress that has been made, the school still struggles with violence. Recently, two gang factions jumped some of her students as they dismissed for the day. However, the school's culture has changed dramatically as students engage this pilgrimage to nonviolence and internalize the principles of nonviolence on both personal and institutional levels.

Update: Pastor Victor Rodriguez

Pastor Victor continues to live and minister in the La Villita neighborhood, where he remains the pastor of La Villita community church. He has recently been named as the Executive Director of Chicago Youth Boxing Club, a neighborhood youth development organization. His passion remains the development of indigenous leadership.

No Ordinary Communion

"And the deepest level of communication is not communication, but communion. It is wordless. It is beyond words, and it is beyond speech, and it is beyond concept. Not that we discover a new unity. We discover an older unity. My dear, we are already one. But we imagine that we are not. And what we have to recover is our original unity. What we have to be is what we are."

- Thomas Merton

I never fully grasped the significance of Communion until I started attending church in my neighborhood. I attend Lawndale Community Church which is an ethnically and economically diverse church. Finding an ethnically diverse church in a segregated city is challenging, finding an ethnically and economically diverse church is even harder. For most of my life, I had gone to a homogenous church. Most of the people had the same skin color, economic level, and political affiliation as I did. In seminary, I learned this fit into a larger strategy by church planters called the "Homogenous Unit Principle." The reasoning is churches will grow faster and bigger if they are made up of one homogenous group. The unintended result is that racial reconciliation is sacrificed on the altar of numerical growth.

When I was visiting my old college church after being in Chicago for a couple of years, I realized how homogenous it was. We were taking Communion and I couldn't understand why it felt different. Then I looked around and everyone looked the same: young, white, and middle class. Communion was a personal experience of grace for personal sins and that was all.

At my church in the city, Communion takes on social as well as personal significance. We have African American, Caucasian,

Latino, Native American and Asian members. There are doctors, single moms, men in recovery, those working for city government and those who can't find jobs, all worshipping side by side. Although we have a wide range of differences, we all stand together in need of grace at Communion. The world creates hierarchies in our society based on color, class, and creed. The Christian church has even been complicit in perpetuating and authorizing these divisions at times. But Communion is a sacrament that screams against these social hierarchies and divisions. "There is neither Jew nor Gentile, neither slave nor free, nor is there male and female, for you are all one in Christ Jesus."[5]

At the heart of Communion is Jesus' prayer in John 17 becoming a reality: that we might become one as God is one. Gilbert Bilzekian, a professor and cofounder of Willow Creek Community Church, describes the unity of God as "a community of oneness."[6] In the Godhead, there is no domination and there is unity within diversity. Jesus' prayer is that we – the church, the Christian community, and I believe the world – would be a community of oneness in this same way.

Being in a church with economic and ethnic diversity highlights the power of the gospel to unite us across all earthly barriers. Communion is not only a personal experience for individual sins, it is a communal experience that shatters social walls and heals social wounds.

Bridges

"We build too many walls and not enough bridges."

- Isaac Newton

Bridges are really a fitting analogy for the work of reconciliation. They allow us access to views we do not normally see. Bridges are connectors between two areas that do not directly touch. Bridges span distance and deep divides. As reconcilers, we are called to be relational bridges between divided people and communities. Paul became a relational bridge between Jews and Gentiles. Like bridges, Paul was stretched to capacity to hold the two communities together. He became a connecting point between two communities that misunderstood and distrusted one another. Through his efforts, Jews and Gentiles were able to find common ground and build community. Bridges can be powerful channels for transformation.

One of our yearlong volunteers really showed me the power of relational bridges. Haley did Mission Year in 2006 in Chicago. During the year she fell in love with the West Garfield Park community where she lived and served. She also deeply loved her college town of Alma, Michigan. Alma was only four hours away from Chicago, yet racially and economically, these two communities were worlds apart. She wanted to bring these two worlds together so she pitched me an idea. She wanted to take a group of youth from Chicago to her college town, but with a twist. The youth from Chicago would be the leaders of her college church's summer VBS program. So, I wanted to get this right: we would send a team of African American youth from the city on a mission trip to the suburbs so they could lead a VBS for wealthy white kids? I thought it sounded crazy enough that it just might be a kingdom idea! Our youth are often seen as recipients of mission, rather than capable and strong leaders. Haley saw the potential of these youth to be ambassadors to her community in Michigan to break down stereotypes, span the divide, and bring these two worlds together.

We had never done anything like this before, but the concept was so intriguing I said "yes." I had so many questions and concerns: would the youth would be accepted, would white parents trust them with their kids, would the youth feel uncomfortable being in a wealthy neighborhood, and how would seeing such extravagance affect them? No one could have expected what happened.

The youth stayed in homes of church members and friends of Haley. The host families fell in love with the youth and the youth felt right at home with their host families. It is what naturally happens when we are not separated from one another. The youth worked hard that week at VBS and the VBS kids loved them too.

That week started a chain reaction. The church members in Michigan decided to continue a relationship with the youth and their church in Chicago. They would have choir exchanges, each church taking turns traveling the 8 hours roundtrip. Some of the host families visited the youth and saw the neighborhood and housing situations in which the youth were living. The town in Michigan has a college and some church members decided these youth deserved to receive the same kind of education as kids who grow up in the suburbs, so they collected scholarships for the youth to go to college.

After the year was over Haley decided to stay in Chicago and keep attending the church in West Garfield Park. She has continued to take youth to lead the VBS in Michigan for the last six years. All of this happened because Haley chose to become a bridge.

I have noticed that the closer people get to those who are different from them, the more stereotypes fade away. We tend to demonize, fear, and misunderstand people we do not know. The closer we get to different communities the more human they become, the more commonalities emerge, and the more our ignorance melts away. Relational bridges are willing to take the risk and reach out because deep down they are convinced that the gospel is the only power able to bring the world together.

Update: Haley Underwood

After her Mission Year in 2006-07, Haley continues to work with Chicago's youth as a Chicago Public School teacher. Haley also continues to mentor youth in her Mission Year church by leading them on empowering summer trips to Alma, Michigan. Mission Year transformed Haley's life, as she now follows her passion to empower youth and children and share God's love with her neighbors.

Being the Church in Boystown

"It's the Holy Spirit's job to convict, it's God's job to judge, and it's my job to love."

- Billy Graham

Boystown is a neighborhood in Chicago with a large LGBTQ population. Every year, Boystown hosts the Gay Pride Parade and thousands of people, gay and straight, line the streets to take part. Although I have been doing ministry in Chicago for awhile, I had never been to the Gay Pride Parade. I had only heard stories from friends as to what goes on.

My conservative friends warned me that it is simply a celebration of raw sexuality. My liberal friends cautioned me to watch out for Christian protesters who hold up hateful posters condemning gays to Hell. I decided to check it out to see for myself.

The reality was actually very different. I did not find the parade to be a celebration of sexuality. I saw floats with gay professionals, gay police officers in uniform, gay military men and women who had served in different branches of the armed services, and gay-friendly politicians soliciting votes. I saw marching bands, social clubs, corporate businesses, dance troupes, jugglers, and many bright colored costumes. Of course, there were a few outrageous outfits, but the majority were tame and respectful. Overall, I saw fellow human beings with a diverse range of interests and skills who desired to be treated equally.

I didn't see Christians spewing hatred to the crowds either. In fact, I didn't see a single protestor, even though I heard a few were there. What I saw pleasantly surprised me. Churches marching in the parade letting the crowds know they would be welcomed at their churches. One church along the parade route had a table out front with cold water for passersby who waited in the scorching summer heat. Another church opened their doors and allowed the crowds to use their bathrooms. Overall, I saw the church being the church in tangible and loving ways to the gay community in Boystown.

I wonder if it is possible to keep from demonizing those we disagree with, especially when it comes to the issue of sexual orientation. I wish we could have a healthy dialogue within the church and with those outside the church. What if the church listened to how the gay community has been hurt by the church? And what if the gay community gave Christians a chance to show we are not all judgmental, mean-spirited people?

What if our stance on this issue was love and we took each person on an individual basis listening to their story, helping address their wounds, and accepting them in our churches as they are (the same way Jesus accepts us)? What if we treated people like human beings created in God's image, loved them as Christ loves us, and let the Holy Spirit do the convicting.

I don't think this is a conservative or liberal response, is it? I think the church needs to stop responding as conservatives or liberals on this issue anyway, and start responding as Christ would. Can we put people ahead of our politics, reconciliation ahead of rhetoric? Or will we let our differences rise above our Christian call to love?

The White Struggle?

"We need to give each other the space to grow, to be ourselves, to exercise our diversity. We need to give each other space so that we may both give and receive such beautiful things as ideas, openness, dignity, joy, healing, and inclusion."

- Max de Pree

An inquisitive senior high school student that my wife and I have grown really close to in our neighborhood asked us a provocative question during a tutoring session. Teshauna had been taking an African American studies course at school which led us into a deep discussion on the struggle of African Americans throughout the history of America. In the middle of our conversation, she paused, looked at us intently and asked, "What is the white struggle?"

The innocent and direct nature of the question caught me off guard. I'm sure I looked like a deer caught in the headlights. Living in a majority African American neighborhood has a way of reminding me of my whiteness. This was one such moment.

But I was also touched by her question, because I knew that she truly wanted to know and understand the pains and struggles of white people in America (this eagerness to know the story and struggle of others is at the heart of racial reconciliation). It was a teachable moment, for all of us. Luckily, my wife was ready.

She explained how many whites had immigrated to America to flee persecution, famine, and poverty. Many white immigrants from Southern and Eastern Europe faced discrimination from other whites upon arrival and were treated as second class citizens. As a former Irish Catholic, my wife shared specifically about how many white Catholics were treated badly because they did not belong to the white Protestant majority.

She shared how the creation of race and whiteness led many to lose their cultural heritage. Instead of being German American or Swedish American, people were lumped into the category of white. As a result of this, many white folks feel like they have no culture.

She explained that today the white struggle is largely related to class. The white poor, who make up the majority of the poor in America, continue to face struggles scraping to get by. Even though I am very aware of the systemic privileges that my skin confers on me – in areas like education, employment, healthcare, wealth, politics, judicial system, life chances, to name just a few – I am also aware that it is important to acknowledge the historical and present struggles whites experience too. So I guess I am learning that I do not have to ignore my own struggles to actively fight against racism, but to be as eager as Teshauna to listen to the struggles of others that are different from me.

Teshauna Edwards

Teshauna has lived in Lawndale all 23 years of her life. Her experience in grammar school seeing dedicated teachers get into the neighborhood and help students learn, inspired her to want to become a teacher. She found a love for music after being part of the Celestial Ministries drumline as a participant and then as a drumline leader. She is now in college at Northeastern University studying music education and wants to work with children with special needs.

CHAPTER SIX

RADICAL HOSPITALITY:
ENCOUNTERS OF COMMUNITY AND SERVICE

"Love seeks one thing only; the good of the one loved. To love another is to will what is really good for him…I must become convinced and penetrated by the realization that without my love for them they may perhaps not achieve the thing God has willed for them…My love must be to them the 'Sacrament' of the mysterious and infinitely selfless love God has for them."
- Thomas Merton

"We cannot seek achievement for ourselves and forget about progress and prosperity for our community…Our ambitions must be broad enough to include the aspirations and needs of others, for their sake and for our own."
- Cesar Chavez

Urban neighbors have a lot to teach us about community. Community is a grace that shows us that we belong to one another and have much to learn from each other. Community reminds us of our responsibility to each other. We sustain community through mutual service. In community, we find ways to give and receive from one another. God is revealed in our service to each other in community.

Radical Hospitality

"The love of one's country is a splendid thing. But why should love stop at the border?"

- Pablo Casals

I have learned radical hospitality from neighbors in my city and other Mission Year cities. In every city where we have placed teams we have stories of neighbors offering hospitality and care for our volunteers. In New Orleans, a house of girls never worried about their safety because their neighbor, an older African American man, reassured them that if anyone gave them any trouble he had their backs. A neighbor in Chicago bought our team a window A/C unit when they heard their apartment didn't have one. In Philly, church members brought by a year's supply of dish detergent because they know the teams are on a limited budget. I seriously have heard story after story where neighbors have come through for our volunteers. In Atlanta, Chicago, Philly, and Houston we have seen volunteers get invited over for meals, welcomed into churches, and included into community events. In each city I have witnessed this same phenomenon, this same grace. This might well be one of the most underreported realities of urban America!

One team that was placed in La Villita (Spanish for Little Village), a predominantly Mexican neighborhood in Chicago, experienced the hospitality of the neighborhood right away. As they pulled up on their first day, they were greeted by a host of friendly faces including kids who ran out to help them carry their luggage up three flights of stairs into their apartment. I always ask our volunteers, "How would these same neighbors be treated if they were moving into your home towns? Would it be the same?" The answer is typically no. Carlos, an immigrant from Mexico who volunteers as a crossing guard to help kids walk safely to school, talked to me about the contrast between American and Mexican hospitality. He said, "If you came to Mexico, you would be welcomed, invited to dinner, and embraced by every member of the family." I have experienced this in traveling to South America. One family in a shantytown in Buenos Aires, Argentina prepared a lavish feast (asado) with chicken, ribs, and steak for me and a coworker who went to visit. Our friends told us that the family did not have a lot of money so their hospitality was literally very costly for them. I can only imagine what it must be like for immigrants that know and expect that kind of hospitality to receive hatred, fear, rejection, and animosity when coming to our country. According to the Billy Graham Center, less than one in ten immigrants will ever be welcomed into the home of an American.[1] How heartbreaking is this when we have such rich resources for the practice of hospitality.

Scripture clearly talks about hospitality. "You must not mistreat or oppress foreigners in any way. Remember, you yourselves were once foreigners."[2] Hospitality gives us the opportunity to welcome the strangers in our midst and remember our own foreignness. We are a nation of immigrants. Besides Native Americans, all of our ancestors came to this country as immigrants. If we are going to welcome the stranger, we will need to try to understand what it feels like to be the stranger. I was impacted when my friend Guillermo (Billy) told me his story of coming to the U.S.

from Guatemala. Although he came from a middle class family in Guatemala, he chose to live and work among low wage immigrant construction workers in California. He lived in substandard housing and experienced the mistreatment many immigrants face. He discovered that many immigrants endure these conditions in order to save money to send back home to their families. He also learned that many immigrants are taken advantage of by employers, withheld wages, and forced into debt slavery. Billy knew that he could leave anytime, but many immigrants do not have that choice. God taught Billy a lot through this experience, mainly not to make assumptions about people before you get to know them and hear their stories. Billy doesn't think immigrants should be pitied, but respected for what they go through to get here, for learning the language, and providing for their families. Billy thinks every person from the U.S. should experience what it's like being an outsider in another country; to not know the language, customs, rules, laws. It can be a humbling experience. I went with Billy to South America and I was dependent on him to translate for me. Billy gracefully interpreted for me letting me in on the cultural cues and jokes I missed. I felt very helpless being the outsider and not knowing the language. It made me really appreciate Billy and those who are bilingual.

I have heard people say, "They need to learn English," referring to immigrants who come to the U.S. I have even heard followers of Christ express this sentiment. I want to say to those people, "If you feel so strongly, then why don't you teach them. Why don't you volunteer at an ESL class and take time to walk alongside an immigrant or refugee." So much of our attitude toward immigrants is simply fear and bigotry hidden behind concerns for national security. When we show this kind of attitude we show that we have not yet been formed by grace.

Jesus showed hospitality to those society considered unacceptable and of low social status. Jesus welcomed himself to Zaccheus' house and ate and drank with "tax collectors and sinners." Jesus also commanded his disciples to welcome the stranger as Christ himself.[3]

God is a God of welcome, a God of hospitality. Receiving the grace of hospitality changes us into hospitable people. As we open our homes and tables to outsiders we become transformed into people of welcome and children of God.

Update: Guillermo "Billy" Quezada

In 2005, Guillermo moved to Los Angeles and connected with a multi-ethnic church plant in South Central LA. During his time there, he met his wife Sarah (Mission Year alum 2001-2002) and they relocated to Atlanta, Georgia in 2009 where he started a bilingual music ministry, Firetongue Music Studio. In 2011, Guillermo served in Buenos Aires, Argentina, leading and training a Mission Year team. Guillermo has taught at churches in Mexico, Honduras, Guatemala, and Argentina. He is comfortable teaching in English or Spanish. Billy is now a General Manager for two car washes in Atlanta and God is constantly teaching him new lessons.

Neighboring

"Next to the Blessed Sacrament itself, your neighbor is the holiest object presented to your senses."

- C. S. Lewis

At Mission Year, we use the phrase "neighboring" to describe the act of being an intentional neighbor. Even though Jesus clearly calls us to love our neighbor as ourselves,[4] many of us still do not even know our neighbors. If we do not interact with our next door neighbors, how are we going to be ready to respond to the "neighbors" that Jesus describes in the parable of the Good Samaritan,[5] those who are alienated and in need?

Our pastor, "Coach" Wayne Gordon, did a 25-week sermon series on "Who's My Neighbor?" Each Sunday he went over another characteristic of who the man in the parable of the Good Samaritan could be. Our neighbor is the one who is beaten, sick, neglected, etc. Week after week we learned another characteristic of who our neighbor was. By the end of the series the congregation was thinking, "Ok we get it, everyone is our neighbor!" That was the point, to live and love as if everyone is your neighbor.

Our neighbors are those on the other side of town that we never cross paths with and those that live next door. Our neighbors are the people we choose to have in our life and those that look, act, and vote differently than us. Our neighbor is the drug dealer hustling to survive and the police officers trying to clean up the streets. Our neighbor is the woman who sells her body on the corner and the little girl who passes by her on the way to school.

Relocation is one way Mission Year practices neighboring. By moving into the community as neighbors, we are able to make the needs of the neighborhood our own. We introduce ourselves and weave ourselves into the life of the community. But neighboring is not only for those who relocate; anyone can be a good neighbor wherever they are. Because of gentrification, the return of the middle class and upper class to the cities, the poor are being displaced, pushed out into the suburbs and surrounding rural communities. Immigration patterns have changed too. Where once immigrants were heading to major cities, now they are moving into more rural areas and smaller cities.[6] This creates an amazing opportunity for all of us to practice neighboring in our cities, whether we live in cities with populations of one thousand or one million.

Neighboring is still a deliberate choice to step across the boundaries of my property to strike up conversation. Sometimes I just make excuses to be outside. I will pick up trash in my front yard, water the flowers, and say "hi" to people who pass by our house. When I see other neighbors outside I will take advantage of the opportunity to have some interaction. We had one Mission Year team in East Garfield Park get creative to get to know their neighbors and fix a pesky problem at the same time. On their way to the bus stop, they noticed a huge bush that was blocking the sidewalk and forcing everyone to walk in the street to get around it. They decided to go door to door and ask neighbors if they had some cutting shears. They purposely went to Jay's house last, because they knew he would have them and wanted to have an excuse to stop and meet their other neighbors along the way. They borrowed the shears from Jay and cut down this wild bush which was a blessing to the whole neighborhood. Finding creative and strategic ways to connect with neighbors and be good neighbors is what neighboring is all about.

Neighboring is a way we create beloved community. Meeting as neighbors is meeting as equals. It enables bonding. Neighbors experience life together. When our neighborhood got 18 hours of nonstop rain and our basement flooded, we were able to experience that with others on our block that also had their basements flooded. When we had a giant hailstorm that pelted all the cars we knew we were not alone. When the lights went out on our block it affected us too and we were able to call the city to get everyone's lights back on. When someone needs a ladder we loan ours out. When we need a car wash or some help in our yard we know there are people on the block who are willing to help us out. When the cops bust someone on the block or the ambulance comes again for the woman across the street, we all feel it together. One day, I was at one of our Mission Year houses and a neighbor's house was on fire. We ran outside and stood with others as the firemen doused the house. We stood there speechless as a mother came running toward the house screaming hysterically for her baby. We were all relieved to find that her baby had been rescued from the flames by a family member. Neighboring allows us to engage more fully in the joys and struggles of our neighbors. We meet on common ground, we share common experiences, and we find a common grace.

Stoop Sitting

"Everything that slows us down and forces patience, everything that sets us back into the slow circles of nature, is a help…an instrument of grace."

- May Sarton

Different cultures have different concepts of time. Some cultures prioritize being punctual and being on time, while other cultures are more event-oriented. Early on, I would show up at exactly the time I was told to meet up and end up waiting for 45 minutes for the next person to arrive. After awhile, I realized that those in my African American community did not have as rigid a view of time as white culture. I've grown to appreciate the difference. I realized that sometimes I can be a slave to time which closes me off to relationships and God and therefore miss out on meaningful interactions with people.

Many of my neighbors in Chicago like to sit on the stoops of their porches. It is a way to escape the heat, but also a way to pass the time. Stoop-sitting challenges the mainstream view of time. Time is money as they say. Because we find our worth in how productive we can be, we pack our days with as much activity as possible, even to the detriment of our health or families. Our lives are shaped by the values of the economy and capitalism which prioritize values of efficiency, productivity, and monetary gain.

Stoop sitting flies in the face of all of those. Sitting on the porch is a very inefficient use of time. But where do we get the idea of efficiency being our highest ideal? Stoop sitting is not productive. Nothing tangible is accomplished. But who says that our lives are measured by how much we produce? Stoop sitting is not about monetary gain. But how did we come to believe our value is in how much money we make? These are false markers for finding meaning and purpose in life.

Stoop sitting is counter-cultural to mainstream culture. It is a way of being present in the moment and being present to those around us. Henri Nouwen talks about prayer as "being useless before God." In God's presence, we do not have to be efficient or productive or successful to gain acceptance. Our value is not in our results, whether they are effective or poor. The way of prayer is to just be with God. Stoop sitting is about just being with another, just being in the moment. Sometimes we mistake frantic activity for missions, rather than just being and communing with one another. Faith and intimacy are built as we allow ourselves to be useless before God and each other. Stoop sitting can be a means of resisting cultural lies. It reveals our false identities and leads us to where meaning is really found. I've learned doing nothing can be a discipline.

Here's what Elsa, one of our volunteers in Chicago, wrote about her sacred moments on the front porch.

"The best thing about living here in Roseland has got to be our front porch. In and of itself, it's nothing special. Just a set of steps and a small landing, wooden boards painted gray. But when you couple a porch with great weather and a house on Skid Row,[7] then great things happen.

There are the kids that come swarming at the door, begging for games and coloring books. There are the neighbors sitting on their porches who wave and say 'hi' to us. Ms B. next door who calls out in her grandmotherly voice to us, 'Hey baby!' J, who rents a room in Ms. B's house, is a Christian who gave up the drug life. He talks about Jesus and prayer with the older boys on the block. D, Ms. B's daughter, who is loud and curious. We go to her for all the news on the block. She talks a mile a minute. M on the other side of us, who asks us to pray for him but isn't ready to come to church with us yet. We hear Mr. B's booming voice on the street. He lives across and a little farther down from us. He can monologue for 2 hours straight.

I like to perch on the railing of our porch and watch the bustle, or read and write there. Sometimes Josh will sneak up behind me and pretend to push me off. He says it's too tempting. Chelsea always comments on how tiny I am. Looks like I'm the only one in the house small enough to sit on the railing. Everyone else sits on the steps or upturned crates.

Every day there's something new on the street; a woman selling candy bars yelling, 'What kind of candy is this? This is BIG-ASS CANDY!' This makes my team crack up. We buy 6 bars, and we decide it's better not to ask where she got them in the first place. On a slow day, one of the drug dealers sweeps up the cigarette butts and trash in front of our house for us. J plays Bryan Adams on repeat in a van. I come home to the smell of barbeque and a constant stream of strangers heading for the free food on the block that the drug dealers are grilling. Chelsea and I munch on wings on Ms. B's porch.

Sometimes I get weird looks because people have such a hard time believing I live in the house. I wonder what they must think when our whole house is on the porch – 2 Black people, 3 White people, and an Asian all living together. I guess it would look a little weird anywhere. But our neighbors are getting used to us, and we are getting used to them. Whoever decided that houses should have front porches was a genius."

Stoop sitting is really about people. It is much better with someone else. On the stoop, you talk life, sports, faith, race, politics, family. You see people pass by and make conversation. Stoop sitting prioritizes relationships which is where we gain real meaning. The stoop is a seemingly timeless place where you forget about schedules and deadlines and just be. It is where you learn the beauty of hanging out. It is where life happens at its own pace.

Update: Elsa Lee

After working with urban youth in Chicago during Mission Year in 2011-2012, Elsa is now in seminary to pursue a career in counseling to better serve the youth in her city. She continues to mentor youth and strives to teach them to learn to see beyond their own world and find a greater compassion for their neighbors.

God takes Public Transportation

"God is always coming to you in the Sacrament of the Present Moment. Meet and receive God there with gratitude in that sacrament."

- Evelyn Underhill

Kayla, a Mission Year team member serving in the Hunting Park neighborhood in Philadelphia, shares how even mundane moments like waiting at the bus stop can become opportunities for building deep community bonds:

"The first time I ever walked to my bus stop to go to my service site, I noticed a mother and her daughter standing together. I think I made eye contact, said good morning and then stood by myself. When the bus came, they kissed each other on the cheek and the girl got on the bus and the mother walked away. This pattern repeated almost every day for about six weeks. Some days just saying 'good morning' turned into small talk, usually about the weather. Six weeks into my Mission Year I was leaving for a weekend long solitude retreat. I had to take my bag of clothing with me to the bus stop because I had to leave right after work. When I got to the bus stop with my bag, the woman pointed to it and asked me if I was leaving. I reassured her and said no, and explained that I'd just be gone for the weekend. Then she said, 'Good, my daughter and I were worried!'

This was when our relationship changed. Once I returned from the retreat we talked every morning. I learned their names, Waleska (the mom) and Valerie (her daughter). Valerie and I began to sit next to each other on the bus when we could. Valerie started asking me questions about college (she's in tenth grade) because her school did not teach her anything about the process. We talked about applying to colleges, financial aid, how she wants to go to a big school and I went to a really small one, things like that. After a week or two talking about college, Waleska sent me a text asking if I could come to their house to help her other daughter, Janice (who is a senior in high school) with her college applications. I went over to their house and walked Janice through the Common App and helped edit her entrance essay.

Janice and Valerie dream of going to college. In my neighborhood, so many kids don't even expect to graduate, let alone go to college. I admire how Waleska encourages her children to dream and to fight to make those dreams happen. She single-handedly moved her family from Puerto Rico to Philadelphia about eight years ago.

The relationship I have with this family has been a true blessing for me this year. Before I left for Christmas break, Valerie brought me a huge bag of home-made cookies. On a particularly cold day this winter our bus was running late, so Valerie and I walked together through a foot of snow to get to the subway. For my birthday, Valerie made me cupcakes and gave me two boxes of tea. This family takes care of me.

Valerie and I agreed that we weren't expecting to make a friend at the bus stop, and we also agree that we're so glad it happened."

It's beautiful seeing relationships form even in unexpected moments like waiting for the bus. It's a great reminder to slow down and take notice where God may be at work in all the moments of our day.

Update: Kayla Aronson

After studying religion at Lewis & Clark College in Portland, Oregon, Kayla switched coasts to do Mission Year in the Hunting Park neighborhood of Philadelphia in 2013-2014. Kayla works as an Intern Residential Service Coordinator at Project HOME's Kairos House, a permanent supported living facility for adults with a history of homelessness and severe mental illness. Kayla believes that treating each other with dignity is at the heart of how Jesus calls us to love, and she hopes her life is a reflection of this. She will be serving a second year with Mission Year as an alum leader.

Taking the Towel

"Oh, the stoop of the Redeemer's amazing love! Let us, henceforth, contend how low we can go side by side with Him, but remember when we have gone to the lowest He descends lower still, so that we can truly feel that the very lowest place is too high for us, because He has gone lower still."

- Charles H. Spurgeon

Everyone wants to be considered a servant but nobody wants to do the dirty work of serving. In the movie *Gandhi*, there is a powerful scene between Gandhi and his wife after they establish an egalitarian commune to experiment with living out principles of equality and nonviolence. Gandhi's wife is mortified to discover that she is expected to clean the community outhouse like everyone else. This is considered the work of untouchables. She appeals to Gandhi that she should not be required to do such degrading work since she is his wife. He gently responds, "There is no work beneath us."

As Christians this should be our motto. Jesus said, "Whoever wants to become great among you must be your servant."[8] For years I tried to embrace this philosophy by cleaning the bathroom whenever I used a public restroom whether it was a fast food restaurant, Starbucks, or gas station (gas stations were always the worst!). In our society, the service sector jobs are often reserved for those on the bottom of the economic food chain. This means more often than not, the poor end up serving the powerful. Often the more money you make the less you have to serve. Jesus flips it. In the kingdom, those who serve are the greatest. So who would Jesus say are the greatest in our society? Who are the ones serving?

King said, "Anybody can be great, because anyone can serve."' The city provides unique opportunities to develop greatness through service. One example stands out in my mind as the kind of service Christ calls us to. Carter, one of our Mission Year team members in Chicago, worked at Breakthrough Urban Ministries, a Christian transitional shelter for men and women. His story describes the sacrament of service in the spirit of Christ. He wrote about it in his journal:

"I watched as Johnny was trying to get himself and his wheelchair into the bathroom. I was then distracted by the request of another guest. A few minutes later he came out of the bathroom. He wasn't able to get situated in time to use the toilet. Other guests and staff quickly noticed the smell and the trail of urine and blood following from Johnny's wheelchair.

Johnny sat helplessly as Teresa (coworker) and I figured out what to do. She got the mop; I went back to get clean clothes from the clothing closet to replace the soiled ones. Teresa asked me to help him get showered. I knew I was about to do something I've never done before. With the clothes and three towels I went with Johnny to the showers.

After getting Johnny out of his chair and into the shower, I helped him get his clothes off. He was so skinny and weak. With the removal of each piece of clothing, he unveiled another layer of vulnerability. Under his shirt was a weak and skinny body; under his shoes and socks were swollen feet with missing toes; Under his shirt hanging out of his side was part of his intestines the size of a fist; his privates were covered with fleshly sores. His mat in his seat was soaked with urine and blood.

I thought, I bet Lazarus' mat in the parable of the rich man and Lazarus must have looked and smelled a lot like Johnny's and a lot less like the clean looking yoga mat I had imagined.

I felt so close to Jesus' ministry I thought of the kinds of people Jesus healed-they were the ones people avoided. Like Lazarus, Johnny couldn't walk. Like the leper, he was infected with sores. Like the hemorraging women, he suffered from bleeding. Yes, the smell was awful and the sight unpleasant, but I remembered Jesus saying 'Whatever you do unto the least of these you do unto me.' And I knew this very well may be the closest I've ever been to serving Jesus."

Update: Carter Sapp

After serving with Mission Year in East Garfield Park in Chicago from 2010-2011, Carter is now completing a Master of Divinity from Truett Seminary at Baylor University and hopes to work as a hospital chaplain. As he continues to pursue the call to come alongside others in difficult times, Carter is continually shaped by the neighbors he grew to know and love in Chicago.

CHAPTER SEVEN

MARCHING IN THE LIGHT OF GOD:
ENCOUNTERS OF RESISTANCE AND PROTEST

*"Protest is when I say I don't like this. Resistance is when I put an end to what I
don't like. Protest is when I say I refuse to go along with this anymore. Resistance
is when I make sure everybody else stops going along too."*
- Ulrike Meinhof

*""Never be afraid to raise your voice for honesty and truth and compassion
against injustice and lying and greed. If people all over the world...would do this, it
would change the earth."*
- William Faulkner

As we see the world as a beloved community we are moved to resist
anything that keeps us divided or threatens the dignity of people. The
city brings us face to face with injustices that we can't ignore. We are
invited to resist forces of evil and protest injustice that dehumanizes
ourselves, our neighbors, and our enemies. Protest gives us the gift of
voice to stand up for ourselves and others experiencing injustice.

Marching in the Light of God

"Even when folks are hitting you over the head, you can't stop marching. Even when they're turning the hoses on you, you can't stop."

- Barack Obama

There's an African proverb that says, "When you pray, move your feet." Marching is a form of prayer and protest. During the civil rights movement, marches were a major tactic for building momentum and advancing the cause of equality and justice. Integrated coalitions would link arms and march together through segregated communities, calling out for change. When Martin Luther King Jr. marched in Chicago to highlight housing segregation, he was met with thousands of jeering, taunting white folks. One person held a sign saying, "King would look good with a knife in his back."[1] At one point, King was actually hit in the head by a stone and fell to his knees. Despite the opposition and violence of the crowd, King kept going and the movement kept marching on.

One of the great things about living in a city is that people are still organizing for change and marching for justice. Every May, there is a solidarity march for immigrant rights and workers' rights. It is a powerful symbol of solidarity among diverse peoples. All the voices chant together:

"Si Se Puede!"

"What do we want? Justice! When do we want it? Now!"

"Asian, Brown, Black and White, peoples of the world unite!"

I was touched seeing signs held up by children crying out, "Don't deport my mom and dad." The march brings together people from different traditions and ethnic backgrounds for a common cause. It's a beautiful picture of unity and hope.

Marches bring awareness, empathy, connection, accountability for those in power, and hope in the struggle. I hear about people who get tired of marching and not seeing anything change. But the march is not about seeing an immediate result, it is about equipping and encouraging people for the long haul. It is confirmation that there are many people that share a common concern. We help each other not lose heart. We inspire each other to keep going. It is a reminder that justice is a long walk, but that we can make it if we do it together.

Anton Flores, co-founder of Alterna, a community of Christ followers from the Americas devoted to faithful acts of hospitality, mercy, and justice, goes on a 100-mile pilgrimage with immigrants during holy week each year. One year Anton and his community marched to the Stewart Detention Center in Georgia to protest the unjust detention of Pedro Guzman, a friend of theirs whose wife and child were suffering without him. The march involved praying, singing, and protesting. The march and the community's consistent protest led to celebration when Mr. Guzman was finally released.[2]

Each year, Chicago loses youth to gang violence and shootings. Many times it's innocent young people who get caught in the crossfire and not even youth that are involved in gangs themselves. One summer it was so bad Chicago got the nickname "Chi-raq" because there were more deaths in Chicago than in Iraq during the war. All over Chicago young people were being slain, and it was hitting our neighborhood as well.

My friend Stanley was inspired to do peace marches in our neighborhood. He organized 10 marches throughout the summer and invited different churches to take part. Our drumline led the march, and we would go to the most active blocks and corners. We stopped to pray at the corners and we held up signs and sang chants like, "Stop the shooting, save the children." One of my favorite chants was "Down with dope, up with hope." We had former gang members and drug dealers marching alongside us as well as the new Chicago Police Superintendent. The marches started gaining attention, so the media and our alderwoman even came out.

The most amazing thing for me was how our neighbors responded. We saw people looking out their windows, coming outside their houses, and running out to join us. By having a mass of people and the noise of the drums, we were breaking the silence and fear of violence.

The march sends a message that there are growing numbers that will not tolerate violence in our neighborhood. It is a visible sign of the reality of God's coming shalom. We do not have to live in fear. A new world is breaking forth out of the old. When we walk in this new reality, the kingdom of God comes.

So I keep marching. Not so much to bring about solutions to all the world's problems, but to pray with my feet: to keep marching until the kingdom comes on earth as it is in heaven.

Hip Hop Prophets

"Hip-hop is supposed to uplift and create, to educate people on a larger level and to make a change."

- Doug E. Fresh

There's a Hip Hop church for youth in our neighborhood called "The House" led by Pastor Phil Jackson, author of *The Hip Hop Church*. Their mission is to present the gospel of Christ in a real, practical, holistic and relational way in order to transform the lives of youth living in today's hip hop culture. They believe the gospel can move through any medium and that includes Hip Hop. They promote Holy Hip Hop.

Many churches – both inside and outside the city – don't believe there's anything redemptive about Hip Hop. They would seriously challenge Pastor Phil's claims that Hip Hop can be transformational. That's mainly because you don't hear real Hip Hop on the radio. The stuff that's on the radio is largely created to exploit Hip Hop for profit. The largest consumers of Hip Hop music are white suburban teenagers and many of the record labels who push the stereotypical hip hop are owned by older white men who end up (intentionally or not) selling a distorted view of black culture to white kids.

The roots of Hip Hop was in social protest against the social ills that many were feeling in disadvantaged communities. The best Hip Hop has a strong social message. Conscious Hip Hoppers critique the status quo and systems that oppress people. Holy Hip Hop is about using the medium of hip hop to unashamedly glorify

Christ. The House Church has allowed the power of the gospel to transform Hip Hop culture so that it can transform youth.

The Hip Hop Church goes to the streets where youth are. Youth are not going into the doors of traditional urban churches like they used to. Youth are not connecting with the older generation's style of gospel music and we are losing youth. The Hip Hop church gives youth a visible sign of the invisible kingdom of God where Christ comes to every culture and has the power to redeem it. No culture or people group is unredeemable. That is just bad theology.

Everybody needs the gospel to be put in their own language. That is why we send and support missionaries to translate the Bible in other countries. No one argues that people who speak Hindi need to hear the gospel in Hindi. If the people speak Hip Hop then the gospel must be translated into Hip Hop. That is what the Hip Hop church is doing.

They do not water down the truth in order to speak to the culture. They come hard. Sometimes I have been uncomfortable with the hard line that Holy Hip Hop draws. It's all or nothing. Black and white. You are either walking with Christ or not. In our neighborhood there is no middle ground. We have liquor stores and churches. The choices kids make could literally mean the difference between life and death. Are they going to find an accepting church community that relates with them or are they going to join a gang to find acceptance?

My good friend and neighbor Terence, is a youth pastor in our community and he is also a DJ. He loves Jesus and he loves Hip

Hop. He refers to himself as a redeemed Hip Hopper and he uses Hip Hop to translate some of the deep truths of God to youth. He once had a sermon titled: "Jesus was an MC." He talked about how in Luke 4, Jesus took the Old Testament Scriptures of Isaiah 61 and remixed it for the people. He said "Today these Scriptures are fulfilled." Jesus had a prophetic message of social change that included bringing "good news to the poor" and liberating prisoners. Jesus also got persecuted and killed for speaking truth like MCs do today.

The message of Holy Hip Hop is connecting with youth. They don't have to reject their culture to become a Christian. Christ speaks to them in their language. Christ relates to them because Christ is an MC.

Update: Terence Gadsden

Terence (AKA DJ Rock On) is a redeemed hip hopper who is striving to live out biblical Christianity by learning to love his neighbors. He has been living in Lawndale for the last 11 years working as a youth pastor and mentor at Lawndale Community Church. He is married to Angela Gadsden, a teacher at Little Village Social Justice High School, and he is the father to two beautiful children. He is currently working on a Masters of Divinity from Northern Seminary.

Let Justice Roll Down

"No, no, we are not satisfied, and we will not be satisfied until justice rolls down like waters and righteousness like a mighty stream."

- Martin Luther King, Jr

One night I was studying Amos 5:21-24, a favorite Scripture passage of mine, in preparation for a seminary class. After studying late into the night, I finally went to bed. I was awakened at 5 a.m. by loud knocking on my front door. My landlord was yelling frantically that our bathroom was leaking. I apparently left the faucet running and water was pouring down from our third floor apartment to the second and first floors. Once I awoke, I jumped out of bed and ran to the bathroom to turn the faucet off.

Ironically, the passage I was studying in Amos was the part where God says, "Let justice roll down like water and righteousness like a never-ending stream." I got a visual image of what it would actually look like for justice to roll down like water. It disrupted the status quo (my sleep). It made a noticeable impression (my neighbors could not ignore it). God wants justice to roll down like waters in every aspect of society. It is not trickle down justice. It is a flood. The flood of justice impacted everyone in our building. No one could ignore it or remain apathetic. It required all of us to wake up to take notice and take action.

I remember early when we moved to Chicago seeing a vision in my mind of a huge water tower. The city below was being consumed by fire and people were trying to put out the fire with squirt guns. All this time, the water tower was up above full of water. I realized the water tower was economic and political resources in communities outside the neighborhood. We have enough resources to address the needs and the injustices plaguing poor communities, but they are not making it to all our neighborhoods. I felt God speaking to me that we needed to find ways to get water redistributed from the water tower to the community in need.

One day I awoke to the sounds of sirens and fire trucks. This is not totally uncommon, but I also heard helicopters overhead so I decided to turn on the local news to see if I could figure out what was going on. After flipping through a few channels, I saw the image of a huge fire blazing in a small shopping plaza within walking distance from my house. I looked at the image on the screen and then looked out my window and could see the dark clouds of smoke. I was transfixed on the amount of water that went into putting out the fire. When there's a fire like that, you need a whole lot of water to put out the flames. A garden hose is not going to work.

Our urban communities are on fire.

We need a flood of justice. People. Skills. Resources. Businesses. Investment. Jobs. Affordable housing. Hope. This drives me to speak and act so that God's justice may flow through us into communities fighting injustice. So many organizations and churches are fighting heroically with limited staff and limited resources. I do not know how to bring a flood of justice, but with what I saw in the vision and what I see in my community, I am committing my life to finding out.

PROTEST!

"There may be times when we are powerless to prevent injustice, but there must never be a time when we fail to protest."

- Elie Wiesel

Part of biblical justice is defending the weak against the strong. Micah, one of the 8th century prophets, was outspoken against the exploitation of the poor by the wealthy and powerful. He protested the corrupt practices of wealthy landowners who seized land and houses through fraudulent and violent practices,[3] government officials who perverted justice by taking bribes,[4] and priests and prophets who served their own self-interest rather than serving the interests of the people in their charge.[5]

Micah used graphic language to describe the way the powerful exploited the weak.

"Listen, you leaders of Israel! You are supposed to know right from wrong, but you are the very ones who hate good and love evil. You skin my people alive and tear the flesh off their bones. You eat my people's flesh, cut away their skin, and break their bones. You chop them up like meat for the cooking pot. Then you beg the Lord for help in times of trouble!"[6]

Micah portrays the leaders as predators who devour the poor for their own gain. In contrast, the biblical call laid out by the prophet Isaiah is to: "Seek justice. Help the oppressed. Defend the orphan. Fight for the rights of the widow."[7] PROTEST!

A couple years ago, I went down to Springfield, Illinois with three Mission Year team members and a convoy of buses filled with

Chicago social service workers. We went to the Capital of Illinois to voice our concerns about the proposed budget cuts that would gut vital programs and services for the poor all across the State. Many of the service sites we partner with would lose funding for their programs and be forced to layoff staff. The budgets of social service programs are being cut to the bone and the poor among us are bearing the brunt. The budget cuts would most negatively affect children, seniors, the disabled, the homeless, and the poor. In other words, the most defenseless and vulnerable in our society.

Some of the results of the budget cuts would be:

- 80,000 working parents would lose child care assistance
- Over 40,000 seniors and people with disabilities would lose their home care
- 15,000 foster children would have their support cut in half
- 175,000 people who depend on community mental health services would lose their care
- 56,000 victims of sexual assault and domestic violence would lose support services
- Substance abuse, teen pregnancy and violence and delinquency prevention programs would be cut affecting 463,000 children and teens.
- 190,000 students would lose college scholarships.

On a very hot June day, we marched around Springfield, carried signs, and protested the budget cuts to these vital services. We crowded the steps of the Capital and cried out for a fair budget. It was a prophetic picture. People from all ethnic backgrounds, ages, and economic backgrounds rallying together to defend the most vulnerable in our communities and to protest the gross injustice of the politically powerful.

I guess not much has changed since Micah's day. Those in power continue to take advantage of the vulnerable. It remains to be seen if our protest will accomplish the intended results. We don't know if Micah's protest was successful either. We just know that it was necessary. After all, if we don't defend the weak against the strong...who will?

"But as for me, I am filled with power, with the Spirit of the LORD, and with justice and might, to declare to Jacob his transgression, to Israel his sin." Micah 3:8

"The LORD has shown you, O mortal, what is good. And what does the LORD require of you? To act justly and to love mercy and to walk humbly with your God." Micah 6:8

Voice

"We must always take sides. Neutrality helps the oppressor, never the victim. Silence encourages the tormentor, never the tormented."

- Elie Wiesel

One of the most annoying aspects of city life is seeing the way women are treated by men. Women have to put up with catcalls, honking, and cars following alongside them. It is hard to see anything redemptive about this. It is sexism plain and simple. In other places in our country, sexism often shows itself in more subtle ways allowing the vast majority to neglect any culpability. In the city you see it plainly. And it makes it impossible not to notice and not to respond.

Even in the midst of this deeply entrenched sexism, I have seen how the city can help people find their voice. I have seen reserved and quiet women erupt with frustration. In the midst of such objectification they are forced to speak out. In the city, they often learn about sexism and that they have a powerful voice against it. They learn to speak out boldly against the mistreatment of women.

I had one volunteer, Emily, who was discovering her voice. I encouraged her to speak up loudly when she felt unsafe. I told her she cannot be polite when it comes to guys coming onto her on the street – she could be firm and clear about how she wanted or didn't want to be treated. She began to feel empowered by her voice. She would be with her team and a guy would come up to the team and she would scream out "NO!" and they would leave. One time a car came up to offer them a ride and she screamed out "NO!!" She didn't notice it was a deacon in her church. It gave the church a good laugh, but it was a significant moment because she was recognizing her power and owning her voice.

Women's voices have always been calling out for change in our communities, culture, and country. Jane Adams is a figure in Chicago that represents the voice of justice. She was the first female Nobel Prize winner for her work among the poor and her protest for women's rights. I know many women who have been raising their voices against injustices in our community and country for decades. Mary Nelson is a community organizer who uses her voice to advocate for marginalized communities that are left out of economic opportunity. Kathy Kelly, founder of Voices for Creative Nonviolence, has used her voice to speak out against war and the collateral damage our military involvement has caused to innocent civilians in Iraq and Afghanistan.

During the NATO Chicago Summit in 2012, I saw the power of women's voices at work in the struggle for justice. A group of hundreds of registered nurses gathered to challenge the world leaders in the Daley Plaza. The new mayor tried to deny them a permit to gather but the women did not back down and they would not be sidelined or silenced. Surrounded by hundreds of police officers, the women protested boldly in the plaza. They called for fairness in the tax structure and more funding for those that need it most. They raised their voices against cuts to medical and social services while corporations were being untouched. It has been a grace to be in the presence of so many faithful women who recognize the power of their voice to say "NO!" to injustice and use that voice to call us back to how the world ought to be, a world more like God intended.

Seeing sexism so blatantly in the city has helped many of our volunteers acknowledge it and become more committed to ending it in all its forms. It has led to more understanding of what women in the community and world endure on a daily basis. The only thing worse than injustice is having no voice against it. The only way we can stop sexism in all its forms is to raise our voices together until every sector of society is rocked. The city provides an opportunity to find our voice and join together with the voices of others to bring justice to our world.

Update: Emily Brown

Emily has been attending Kennesaw State University since her Mission Year to learn about nonprofit administration. Her experience in Mission Year right out of high school provided direction and vision for her personal and professional life. Seeing the need for people with patience and compassion in the city has shaped her desire to see God glorified through her profession. She hopes to be a force for change in underprivileged communities by guiding nonprofit organizations with grace, hope, and justice for those without an audible voice.

Voting

"Voting is a civic sacrament."
- Theodore Hesburgh

I never voted before moving to Chicago. Before that time I had not been involved in the political process at all. I am convinced that the main reason that I was not involved in politics earlier was that I did not need to be. As a white, middle class, male Christian I had (and have) plenty of representatives looking after my interests. Since I had my needs taken care of, I did not need to be engaged in the political process. It is a much different story for those in the minority in our country. If you are in the minority, you have to fight for your political voice to be heard. Even when you do vote, you often face obstacles.

I remember talking to a professor from a college in Michigan who brought a group of students to Chicago to expose them to issues of poverty and injustice. He told me that some of their students were hired by a political party to hold up the voting lines in poor, African American districts since it was assumed they would vote against their candidates. I could not believe it. How could Christians seek to suppress the votes of fellow citizens? How could our loyalty be to a political party over the values of freedom and justice? More recently, voter ID laws have been proposed to hinder the elderly and minorities from having their voices heard.

Another obstacle stands in the way of marginalized communities; there is a growing apathy about the political system and process. It is easy for people in my neighborhood to feel like voting does not matter (even middle class folks feel this way). I asked one young adult in our community if she was going to vote now that she was 18 and she said "No, I don't care about politics." I said, "You don't care about our community getting money for our schools, jobs, improvements in our community?" She said, "Well, yeah." I said, "Politics is how we divide up our tax money. If we do not vote then we won't get as many resources into our community." That made more sense to her.

When we realize there are real life consequences for our communities, it is vital that we are engaged in the political process. This is why voter registration drives are so important in our communities. It is not just about politics, it's about empowerment. Voting gives people a voice and a sense of personal power that they have the ability to influence our country's policies. Whether they are voting for our party or not, should not be the issue, we should seek for every citizen's vote and voice to count, otherwise our democracy is a fraud.

In Christianity, there is a tradition of withdrawal and a tradition of engagement in politics. Traditions like Quakers and Mennonites choose to abstain from engaging in politics out of deeply held theological reasons. There is also a tradition of engagement, Christians and churches being actively engaged across the spectrum of parties and issues. I respect those that withdraw because they feel that voting compromises the gospel, but I'm concerned because I hear many young Christians withdrawing for different reasons. I see many young Christians withdraw out of apathy. I believe it is easier to withdraw from politics when our interests are being represented and needs met. In this sense, withdrawal is simply consent for the status quo.

It is possible to be engaged in politics and stay loyal to the gospel over a political party. We must use the gospel to critique each party, candidate, and issue rather than interpret Scripture based on our political leaning. The church loses its moral voice when it endorses a political party uncritically. The church, for the Christian who withdraws or engages politics, is to be a prophetic voice. This means we need to know what is going on, speak truth to power, stand up for the vulnerable, and keep leaders accountable.

I do not vote for myself anymore. I choose to vote differently. I give my vote to those that need it more than I do. I vote for the interests of my neighbors. I do not vote for myself because I am taken care of already. Which candidates have more awareness and concern for the issues and realities of my neighbors? My loyalty is not to a party, but to love God, love my neighbor, make peace, share what I have with the poor, remember those in prison, welcome the stranger, defend the widow and orphan. This is our prophetic call that we cannot forfeit no matter how engaged we are in politics.

Some churches and communities have to fight for their rights as citizens, where others can easily take their rights for granted. Whether you vote your conscience, follow your conscience and refuse to vote, or whether you use your vote for those that need it more than you, be prophetic and not apathetic.

Voting is a sacred act, a right, and a responsibility.

CHAPTER EIGHT

No Hugging in My Courtroom:
Encounters of Justice and Generosity

"A just person is one who is conformed and transformed into justice."
- Meister Eckhart

"The response to war is to live like brothers and sisters. The response to injustice is to share. The response to despair is a limitless trust and hope. The response to prejudice and hatred is forgiveness. To work for community is to work for humanity. To work for peace is to work for a true political solution; it is to work for the Kingdom of God. It is to work to enable everyone to live and taste the secret joys of the human person united to the eternal."
- Jean Vanier

As we learn to resist evil and protest injustice, we are able to become witnesses of God's justice and generosity. Human justice is far from biblical justice. Biblical justice calls us to compassion, to go the extra mile, and to love without agenda. From unjust judges to corrupt cops, fundraisers to food donations, we see how the city invites us to be transformed into more just and generous people.

No Hugging in My Courtroom

"This is a court of law, young man, not a court of justice."
- Oliver Wendell Holmes

Working in communities on the west side and south side of Chicago allows you to see another side of the systems of our society. You get to see how many of these systems are broken and working against people in our community. Much of their lives revolve around navigating these broken systems and trying to keep their lives together even when these systems are tearing them apart.

The criminal justice system is one of those systems. Standing alongside neighbors in the city gives you a whole new perspective on our justice system. We see how our human concepts of justice fall short of the justice God desires for the world. Emily, who served with Mission Year in the Englewood community, shares this eye-opening encounter she had accompanying a friend to court:

"This story starts with my friend Keisha.* Keisha lived down the street from where I and my flat-mates lived in Chicago. Over the course of several months, many of us were very close to her and her family. Keisha was a five-foot-two 38 year-old woman with enough energy and life to light up the entire block. She was feisty and she had a lot of street smarts. She wasn't scared of many things, though she'd seen and encountered plenty. Guns didn't scare her, but butterflies sent her running the opposite direction.

Keisha had a few brothers, three that shared a home with her, her daughter, and her grandmother (her mother had passed away many years before). Her grandmother had raised her and her brothers. In her 70s, she was still working a full-time job, despite her deteriorating health. She was a determined woman with incredible strength, but with enough love that my Mission Year team was welcomed as part of her family, and were immediately told to call her Grandma.

Of Keisha's siblings, two of her younger brothers were arrested in the year that we knew them. One of them was in for a longer-haul, but the other tended to be in-and-out with minor offenses. Her youngest brother, Jared,* was a good friend of mine. He was just a year younger than me and he might well be one of the most upbeat, fun people to be around that I know. He had such a natural charisma and positive demeanor. Everyone loved to be around him.

But things started to spiral. After some time had passed, Jared was also arrested on multiple offenses. My team visited him in jail a few times. It tore me apart to see him in there for the first time. His front two teeth were missing; he told us the cop bashed them in with a flashlight when he was arrested. Despite his missing teeth, Jared still had a warming smile that offered hope.

More and more time passed. My teammates and I went to all of his trials at court that we could make. His public defender almost never showed up to the trials, which led to continuance after continuance. Each time we saw him, his eyes seemed dimmer. He no longer seemed comforted by our presence at the trials. When we visited him in jail, he tried to keep the conversation light, but his eyes told us of things that he kept from us.

On one particular trial, we went with Keisha up to the courthouse. She wasn't doing well. By this point, all three of her brothers were in jail, Grandma was very sick and Keisha was struggling just to maintain her way of life. My friends and I had watched the previous three trials and the judge was coming down hard on each of the offenders. The judge was sick and in a horrendous mood – and she didn't seem to try to keep that from affecting her judgments.

Finally, it was time for Jared's trial. He shuffled out in his jumper. The judge called Keisha to the front and asked her some questions. Keisha seemed nervous. She tried to interact cordially with the judge, but the judge was put off by it and told her to stop talking. The judge then asked her a question which confused Keisha. She tried to answer but she was having difficulty comprehending what was being asked. In response, the judge said something to insult Keisha's intelligence.

From my bench looking on, I was very upset. Who was this judge to treat this incredible, strong, beautiful woman in such a way? The judge was casting judgment not just on Jared, but on his family, on his friends, on anyone who rubbed her the wrong way, and on anyone with less power than her, which happened to be everyone in that courtroom. The trial was postponed yet again, and as Keisha returned to our bench, I was compelled to hug her.

I'm not typically one to initiate physical affection. I know people feel very differently about physical contact and I am cautious not to transgress any boundaries. For Keisha and I, hugging just wasn't something we did. Until that moment. I can't explain it, but for a second I felt what she was experiencing, and it was devastating. So I hugged her. And she cried – something I had never seen her do before or since, even though she had more reason to than many.

Suddenly, she pulled back, apologizing profusely. I was confused for a second, until I regained awareness outside of that moment. I heard the judge's voice and I turned to her seat. She was yelling, 'No, I'm talking to that young lady!' And she was pointing at me. I was so confused. I said, 'What?' She replied hotly (and just as loudly), 'You do not hug in my courtroom! You do that at home! You don't do that in my courtroom!'

I was taken aback. My face flushed with rage. I have only been that angry maybe a total of 5 times in my life. Stunned and angry, I said, 'Sorry.' But I clearly didn't mean it. My heart beat faster, I was shaking with adrenaline, and I could feel the blood pumping in my ears. In the best wisdom I could muster in my anger, I opted to storm out of the courtroom rather than to turn and flip her off. The whole ride back to our place, about an hour to an hour and half commute, I was shaken. My friends who were there asked me if I was okay. They know I cry at a moment's notice and tend to be sensitive. But I was just livid.

Yet Keisha didn't seem phased at all.

I realize that because of my position in the story, because of white privilege, because of my class, because of a flurry of factors, this story was significant to me. Anger was the only natural reaction to have. I felt like I could storm out of the courtroom. I didn't feel the need to make a heartfelt apology to the judge. Whereas Keisha, who is much stronger than me, does not have white privilege, comes from a rough socioeconomic background had been submissive to the powers that be. Not out of acquiescence, but out of wisdom. For little old me, this was one of my first big realizations that justice doesn't necessarily always have a place in the courtroom. Keisha knew. It's the life that she's seen and the life that she's lived. I learned a lot that day.

I am glad I was open to loving her shamelessly. If I regret anything, it is that I apologized to the judge. I think I wish I would have calmly nodded and said 'Ok.' Not apologizing, but not allowing my anger to fight against the beauty of what I felt happened there. I am so grateful for Keisha. And I am grateful for the ways this story changed me. I wish I could put it into words. But for now, this will have to do.

I'll close with a poem I encountered a few years later, which seemed to resonate with me after this experience:

Justice (Langston Hughes)

That Justice is a blind goddess

Is a thing to which we black are wise:

Her bandage hides two festering sores

That once perhaps were eyes."

Emily's experience in court highlights the difference between God's justice and our human justice system. The heart of biblical justice is compassion; the heart of human justice is retribution. Biblical justice includes binding up the broken-hearted[1] and giving a heartfelt hug in a moment of agony. There was no room for compassion in that courtroom and in many courtrooms in our country. When we severe compassion from justice we are no longer talking about biblical justice. Biblical justice means defending people from all that dehumanizes and destroys dignity. Sometimes this means defending people against our own courts of law.

Update: Emily Shakal

Emily stayed in Chicago for three more years, earning a degree in Biblical and Theological Studies from North Park University in 2012. She then moved to North Augusta, South Carolina where she currently works as a laboratory assistant in a neighboring city. When asked to consider Mission Year's impact on her life today, she stated that she is still struggling to find out how to live a congruous life with all the values she claims to have.

The Englewood 5

"Change does not roll in on the wheels of inevitability, but comes through continuous struggle."

- Martin Luther King Jr.

On 26th Street and California Avenue sits a large maximum security prison. It is only a mile and a half from my house, and one morning I biked over to sit in on a hearing at the Cook County Criminal Courthouse. The judge agreed to hear the case on Columbus Day, usually a holiday at the courthouse, to accommodate the attorneys.

The case involved the Englewood 5, five teenagers, who were accused of murder in 1994. New DNA evidence found on the victim actually pointed to a different offender, a serial rapist, who had been convicted of similar crimes during the time of the incident. The defense attorneys were requesting an order to vacate the existing decision and allow for a retrial. The signatures of 65,000 people were collected and handed over urging the release of these men who had served decades in prison for something DNA evidence was showing they did not do.

I sat in the gallery of the courtroom listening to the talented team of New York and Chicago lawyers passionately defend their clients and plead to the judge. Family of the defendants sat in front of me and over 50 supporters turned up to show the judge there was public support.

The heart of the defense was that DNA evidence showed that the semen found on the body belonged to Johnny Douglas, a serial rapist who had a history of assaulting and killing women who engaged in prostitution. They stated that this new evidence would likely lead to a different outcome than the verdict the previous judge had ruled. The matter the judge could not get past was that all five teenagers had confessed and pled guilty to the murder. The attorneys gave examples of many exoneration cases where false confessions were given.[2] The judge and attorneys went back and forth. Finally, the judge said he would need more time to make a decision.

Everyone in the courtroom was expecting a decision that day so naturally there was disappointment and even anger. I learned something though. Justice is not easily won. It is a battle. There's a parable in Luke 18 about a widow and an unjust judge. The widow, who represents the most economically vulnerable in that society, demands justice from an unjust judge. At that time, wives did not inherit their husband's estate. Women and children would often become destitute because they had nothing to live off of. The text says the judge is an unjust judge who did not have fear of God or compassion for people. By law, judges were to decide cases fairly with fear of God. The case does not look good for the widow. But the widow does not accept injustice. She continues to come back day after day demanding justice. She continues with such persistence that the unjust judge is worn down. Judges in that time were known to take bribes to settle cases. That meant those with wealth could get off while the poor were out of luck. The widow did not have money to bribe but she had persistence. In that time, women were not known to represent themselves in court. Her repeated presence was a way of shaming him. Eventually, the judge decided in her favor because he saw that she would not back down.

When the trial for the Englewood 5 reconvened the judge decided in favor of the Englewood 5. My experience in court and studying the parable have taught me a lot about the nature of justice. Justice is not guaranteed. It must be demanded. Not once. Not twice. But repeatedly. Those without resources are often at a disadvantage in the courtroom, but when we stand up as a larger collective and persevere together we can eventually wear down those in power to do what is right.

To Serve and Protect

"Where there are too many policemen, there is no liberty. Where there are too many soldiers, there is no peace. Where there are too many lawyers, there is no justice."

- Lin Yutang

Many of our neighbors do not like the cops. This can be surprising to many newcomers to the city. I grew up in places where the cops would be the ones you called first when you were in trouble. In the city, they are the last resort if they are called at all.

After 10 years in the city, I have to admit I struggle with my view of the police. I see them frequently speeding down the opposite direction of a one way street or running red lights. They can stop you randomly simply for walking or driving in "the wrong neighborhood." Cops make random stops on our block. One time they handcuffed a group of five teenagers together and propped them against the hood of their car outside our apartment. The officer proceeded to check their pockets for drugs. The cop pulled one of the guy's pants down and searched his underwear while the boy stood humiliated in the middle of the street (he didn't have any drugs on him). It is no wonder folks in the neighborhood have anger toward cops.

Even those that come into the neighborhood from the outside can become targets of police harassment. Many of our volunteers have been pulled over by cops for simply walking down the street. Cops assume white volunteers are in the neighborhood to buy drugs which is ironic, because people in the community assume our volunteers are cops. One year, I sent a team of volunteers to the police station to introduce themselves to the local officers to hopefully make the cops more aware of their presence in the neighborhood. I had the team ask the cops for any safety advice. One cop said, "Buy a gun." The cops' view of the neighborhood is as bad as the neighborhood's view of the cops.

Another story involves Ashley, a white volunteer, who was serving in the Lawndale neighborhood with Mission Year. She lived with a team of young women in an apartment building where two men from our church were living. The men were ex-offenders who had gone through our church's recovery program and they made it their personal mission to watch out for the young women who were living in the city for the first time. The team had the guys over for meals and the guys would check in on the team.

Ashley was coming back from her work site when a cop approached her outside the apartment building. He asked her what she was doing there and then started making advances on her and saying very suggestive things. He kept his hand on the door into her apartment to block her from going in. She felt very uncomfortable and finally had to force her way past him and into the apartment. The next day, this cop was waiting for her after work and continued to come onto her.

She told the guys in the apartment building what had happened and they were very protective. They were angry that this cop would abuse his power and they took it personally. They ended up calling the police station and filing a complaint against this cop. After that, the cop did not come around again. Ironically, she felt more protected by the ex-offenders than she did the cops. Just like in Jesus' parables, the heroes in the story are not always the ones you would think.

Safety and protection often come from unlikely places. Those who serve and protect the community are not always the ones in uniform. Of course, there are good cops. Thankfully, not all the cops are like the ones in these stories. But it's hard for folks in our community to trust cops when so many of their experiences have been negative.

These experiences show the abuse of power that can go unchecked in areas of poverty. These are warnings about the way power corrupts. Those with power can take advantage of those who do not have power. As Christians and citizens, we have a collective responsibility to serve and protect the most vulnerable so that our communities can become safe for all people.

Update: Ashley Nienaber

Since living in the North Lawndale neighborhood of Chicago with Mission Year in 2007-2008, Ashley has found that as long as she is living in overlooked places, she is home. After spending 4 years practicing presence in South Atlanta with her husband Mike and two small sons, she and her family now live in South Seattle. There she is challenged daily to see God's movement with fresh eyes- as a stay at home parent, a community advocate, a doula-in-training, and a student of the rich culture her neighborhood has to offer.

Financial Crisis

"The size of a challenge should never be measured by what we have to offer. It will never be enough. Furthermore, provision is God's responsibility, not ours. We are merely called to commit what we have – even if it's no more than a sack lunch."

- Charles R. Swindoll

When the economy tanked back in 2008, many non-profits also suffered greatly. Giving went down and many organizations had to close their doors. Our organization also took a big hit. At one point, it even looked like we may have to close down. We had about 70 yearlong volunteers who were dedicating themselves to living and serving in urban communities with a few months left in their year of service. Our collective fundraising numbers were far from where they needed to be and the outlook was bleak.

Our board set up some goals and deadlines that we needed to hit, otherwise we would have to shut down. We talked with our volunteers about the situation and how important it was that all of us be involved. We committed ourselves to prayer and to strategizing about how to raise enough money to keep going. We decided to take a community approach. We would all work together to raise the money. Those who were low in their fund-raising took time to focus on fund-raising, and those who had raised their money asked their own contacts to support those whose support was low.

For a couple weeks the outcome was unsure. We prayed and prayed. We knew that closing down would be devastating to the communities and organizations depending on our volunteers. Each of our teams voluntarily cut back on their expenses. Everyone made phone calls and emailed their contacts to support their work in the city. All of our teams did local fund-raisers. One of our teams had a spaghetti dinner at their house in the Englewood community. They invited everyone they knew. They did not think many people would come since many of their neighbors stay inside their homes at night due to fear of violence and those who live outside Englewood are afraid to come at any time. They could not have expected what would happen. One of our team members, Corrinn, wrote about the whole experience:

"Another great idea that my team came up with was a dinner benefit that we held last Saturday at our home. Mind you, we only had less than a week to prepare for it and get the word out. We were nervous about the turn out as most folks weren't eager to come spend their Mother's Day weekend with us over a plate of spaghetti. We were also discouraged to hear that some people wouldn't be interested in coming because of the stigma that Englewood has as being a 'dangerous place.' In spite of this, we continued to invite and share with the community our situation and goals, and it was amazing to see how folks jumped to help.

Everyone was eager and willing to contribute in some way. People put our invitation on websites, blogs, and flyers in the neighborhood. I even had the opportunity to promote Mission Year and our benefit on the radio (WVON 1690). Others contributed food and drinks and materials; and those who couldn't make it were sure to give a donation right then and there. Through the benefit, we were able to raise $400!

I was truly amazed at how the Englewood community worked on our behalf. I was reminded of all the times when my team and I were greatly discouraged and distraught because we felt like we hadn't built any relationships in the neighborhood. Well, this event was a testament that our prayers were answered and our efforts were not in vain. It was amazing to watch our efforts be reciprocated!

In the midst of the craziness of that first week, people continued to give, even people I didn't know. For example, some Mission Year Alumni contacted me and donated, then sent a care-package full of goodies just as encouragement. Even someone who heard me on the radio gave me a call and contributed online that same day! And just this morning, I awoke to a note on my dresser from a roommate who donated a part of her income tax refund to get me to the last stretch of my goal! Unbelievable!"

At the end of the year, the team remembered the spaghetti fundraiser as one of their most significant memories from the year. Who would have thought a fundraiser during a financial crisis would lead to one of the year's finest ministry moments.

Seeing neighbors, friends, alums giving to keep Mission Year going gave us even more resolve to not give up. After two weeks, we were able to raise over $25,000 and we didn't stop there. We rallied as a community, everybody doing their part. Houston teams worked concessions at Astros games at night, teams put on concerts, we had alums giving and raising money too. We kept sharing small victories with each other to keep momentum going. We saw an amazing outpouring of support come in. Pedro, one of our team members wrote, "I want to celebrate the fact that God is making Malachi 3:10 true for all of us. We are not putting His name to the test but it is being tested and blessings have already started to come. The blessing for me is this community and the endless possibilities that can come out of it for His glory." Some team members who were lowest in support when the crisis hit ended up exceeding their goals and had the most support by the end of the year. That year brought us together as a city and as a national organization. Economic hardships have a way of turning you into a community of faith. That year also resulted in more people choosing to stay in the city after the program ended than any other year.

It was an amazing moment to see God bring so much good out of a trying time. It was confirmation to us that God wanted us to continue the work in our communities. We learned about God's faithfulness and the power of community. We saw a financial crisis that could have led to panic and fear turn into a sacrament of community, faith, and provision.

Update: Corrinn Cobb

After Mission Year 2008-2009, Corrinn decided to stay in the Englewood community where she has been involved in local activism and community development efforts. She is currently working on a Masters in Community Development from Eastern University. She hopes to start her own line of African American beauty products.

Love Without Agenda

Ko taku rourou
Ko tau rou rou
Ka ora te tangata

With my resources
And your resources
Everyone will benefit

- A New Zealand Maori Proverb

One day I got a phone call at the office asking if we take donations. A fancy hotel in the Gold Coast, the wealthiest area of Chicago, was upgrading all of its linens and wanted to know if we would be interested in taking their old bedding. I jumped at the opportunity knowing that we could definitely find use for it in our community. We borrowed an old church van and headed downtown. When we got there they had hundreds of bags of comforters, sheets, and blankets. We stuffed a 15 passenger van from floor to ceiling and brought the bounty to our neighborhood. We stopped by Hope House, the men's recovery house at our church first.

Some men came out and helped unload and they started sorting all the items. They have 50 beds for men who are coming out of prison or seeking freedom from addiction. We had enough for each bed and still had some leftover so I called up Pat because I knew she would be able to distribute them to families in the community that could really use them. I was overjoyed to think that people in our neighborhood would be sleeping on the same quality of bedding as those in the Gold Coast.

That's when I fell in love with redistribution. When you are redistributing you feel like Robin Hood, taking from the rich and giving to the poor. But in this case, you are taking the excesses of the rich and sharing it with those that don't have access to those same goods. Redistribution is sharing our abundance with those that don't have enough.

Now, anytime I get calls offering donations I jump on it. I want to be a bridge between communities of too much and communities of not enough. People who have, don't always know people that need.

A few years ago, an organization called Love Without Agenda, founded by Jimmy Spencer and Lisa O'Brien-Wentzel, called my wife and I asking if we wanted free groceries from Trader Joe's to distribute in our neighborhood. We didn't have to think long about it. Our neighborhood, like many marginalized neighborhoods in urban areas, is considered a food desert. Food deserts are neighborhoods with limited access to quality grocery stores, affordable food, produce, and healthy options. Without competition from other stores, corner stores can keep prices high and stocked with junk food.

Trader Joe's is an affordable grocery store that has healthy, organic food. The problem is, the closest Trader Joe's is across the city. So every Sunday, we would go to Trader Joe's on the North side to pick up a church van full of groceries. We brought them to our block where we had a team of people unload and sort the food. Then over the next few hours people from our neighborhood would come by and get what they needed. There was always more groceries than we needed so we had friends from different neighborhoods come by and take groceries to share with their neighbors. Even after that, we had bags of food left so we donated the rest to a food pantry at a homeless shelter or a senior center. Food that would normally be thrown out (and many grocery stores do throw away) fed multitudes.

For us it was not just about meeting a need. The groceries were a means of building community among neighbors. Sorting and sharing groceries led to conversations and connections. We were able to meet a lot of our neighbors and hear their stories, which was an answer to prayer for us. The founders of Love Without Agenda have been doing this kind of redistribution for many years, and testify that when we share our resources in this way, we start to create a new economy: God's economy of generosity and community. Sharing builds community which brings life. When we share our resources with one another and love without agenda we encounter a grace that changes us all.

Update: Love Without Agenda

After a year of giving away groceries out of our basement we found a church on the west side that was willing to take it on and better positioned to leverage this resource to the wider community. A retired gentleman in the church is now organizing it and sharing responsibilities for distribution between four different churches and communities. It is beautiful to see resources being shared, church communities working together and the kingdom expanding.

CHAPTER NINE

CHICAGO BLUES:
ENCOUNTERS OF SUFFERING AND LAMENT

"To believe that God is not a being separate from us is to know that God neither causes nor allows the events that comprise our life rather God is one with them, radically present and unconditionally incarnate."
- Tom Stella

"I realized that healing begins with taking our pain out of its diabolic isolation and seeing that whatever we suffer, we suffer it in communion with all of humanity, and yes, all of creation. In so doing, we become participants in the great battle against the powers of darkness. Our little lives participate in something larger."
- Henri Nouwen

The city teaches us to lament. It is easy to romanticize the city, but the city is a place of deep sorrow. When we enter into the suffering of others' pain and injustice, we learn to lament. Lament is a way of expressing the reality of suffering without losing hope. What do we do with the city's dark side? Can God be experienced when our worst fears are realized? We see how God is deeply present in suffering, muggings, scandals, and violent deaths. Even in crucifixion grace is present.

Chicago Blues

"The Blues is Life."

- Brownie McGhee

Chicago is home of the blues. At the end of each year, I take my leadership team to a Chicago blues club. Buddy Guy's Legends, B.L.U.E.S., or Rosa's lounge are a few favorite spots. DJ, a friend and fellow drummer from my church, worked at Rosa's as a bouncer. DJ would always tell me when the good acts were playing and let us in for half the cover charge. DJ and I shared a passion for God, drums, and blues.

Blues music has a way of soothing the soul. The blues are a kind of fellowship of suffering. Blues can be a very lonely experience and a deeply universal, communal one. Sitting in a blues club and feeling the music wash over you can be therapeutic. The blues affirm the pain, disappointment, and longing of life. The listener is given permission to let their wounds be exposed and to express their pain.

Before moving to Chicago, death always seemed distant. Having been here has changed that. Death is close. Since being here, I have attended funerals of babies who died from medical complications and young people who died from gun violence. Trite words like "at least we know they are in heaven now," does not do our grief justice. We feel cheated by death yet we often cheat ourselves out of fully expressing the depths of our agony.

This does not have to be the case, because our Christian faith has a resource for handling the paralyzing loss and perilous suffering: lament. Lament is a way of acknowledging the tragedy without trivializing the pain. In the book of Lamentations, Jeremiah the prophet lets out a soulful cry for the devastation and ruins of the city. David writes songs that sound like they could be on a Muddy Waters album. Chris Rice, Co Director of the Center for Reconciliation at Duke Divinity School, points out that the book of Matthew is bookended by lament. In the beginning it begins with the lament of Rachel's children[1] and then ends with Jesus' lament of "My God, My God, why do you forsake me."[2] The Biblical writers seemed perfectly fine sitting with pain and expressing their agony. They were acquainted with the blues.

Being surrounded by such tragedy can be overwhelming, and many people feel unequipped to handle the losses. A woman who is forced to sell her body to survive dies alone in a park. A six year old girl is shot and killed in a drive-by shooting. An honor student is struck down by a mob of youth who get caught up in the frenzy of territorial dispute. My friend DJ recently passed away, leaving behind his wife and daughter. I attended the funeral and felt the sadness resting in my chest. I know the only way to heal is to let myself feel that pain.

I look at the sorrowful city. I see an unequal education system, an unjust prison system, a broken economic system, dilapidated housing, violence and death. The only response that makes sense in light of these realities is lament. The blues, Chicago, and the bible are teaching me to lament, to name my pain, my powerlessness, my sorrow and to speak them to the God who laments. The God who knows the blues.

Where Thieves Break In

"Your most precious, valued possessions and your greatest powers are invisible and intangible. No one can take them. You, and you alone, can give them. You will receive abundance for your giving."

- W. Clement Stone

My wife and I got a call from our upstairs neighbors that our house had been broken into. When we got the call we were in Atlanta for an annual staff meeting and would not be back in Chicago until two days later. Needless to say, those two days were difficult as we wondered what the condition of our house would be, and which of our possessions would be missing.

When we finally arrived home, we found that our computer was gone along with some other electronics and jewelry. Our place was not trashed which we were grateful for and some of our most treasured things had been overlooked or ignored (luckily journals and books don't do too well at the pawn shop!).

The day we returned was our 10 year wedding anniversary, which we ended up spending on our couch reflecting on what is really valuable in our lives. We thought of the special memories we had as a couple, the time spent with people we love, relationships with our friends and neighbors, mentors that invested in our lives, the struggles and joys of following God's call in the city. None of these things can be taken from us.

Jesus said, "Do not store up treasures on earth where moths and rust can destroy and where thieves break in and steal, but store up treasure in heaven."[3] This is a command many of us Christians do not obey in our consumerist culture. I think Jesus teaches this because our lives can become so consumed with our stuff and how to secure our stuff, that we don't notice our neighbors, especially those that may be struggling on the edge of poverty or in the throes of addiction. As long as there is addiction and poverty, there will be theft. When we got over the initial shock of hearing our home had been invaded, we began to think about the deeper causes that lead people to such desperate measures.

When we store up treasure in heaven rather than on earth, we allow for more equitable redistribution of the resources God has provided all of humanity. We don't hoard, we don't take too much of the earth's resources. When we store up treasures for ourselves, rather than sharing resources with others, we create inequality between ourselves and our neighbors. We also risk missing out on the kingdom moments that money can't buy and thieves can't steal— the stuff eternity is made of.

In some ways, having our house broken into is a kind of city sacrament. It is a common ritual that most other families we know have experienced at least once living in the neighborhood. It forces us to simplify our lives and remember what is most valuable. The experience reveals the attitudes and reactions in our hearts: anger, vengeance, confusion. After the break-in, we decided to voluntarily go through our stuff and try to give away items that we didn't need or that others could use more than us. We wanted to let the incident be a means of grace and change rather than simply a negative moment we tried to forget. It became an opportunity for us to better follow Christ's command and remember where our true treasure lies.

Mugging

"It is to the Cross that the Christian is challenged to follow his Master: no path of redemption can make a detour around it."

- Hans Urs von Balthasar

.

The worst part of my job is getting the call that someone has been mugged. I remember getting a call from Josh on Valentine's Day while my wife and I were on our way out for a date. He had been walking from work when a group of guys came up to him. One guy hit him and another demanded his money. Wisely, he had a five dollar bill rolled up around a one dollar bill in his pocket for just this type of situation and the guys took it and ran thinking they had a lot more than $6. I rushed back immediately to spend the evening with Josh. There's not much you can say in those moments. All you can do is enter into that unsettling space and be there together.

These moments are rare, but they are hard to forget. They take time to process and recover from. It's important to let yourself feel the full range of emotions. It is common to feel anxiety for awhile after an incident. It's vital to give yourself time. Don't be afraid to ask people to accompany you places for awhile.

One time, a volunteer named Jenny was called back to identify a person who had held her up. It can be an intimidating task. We sat together at the police station waiting to go into the room to point out the guy. She struggled with whether she should press charges since she knows the prison system is not the answer. Oftentimes prison makes people more hardened criminals rather than rehabilitated. At the same time, people who are involved in violent crimes or battery need to have consequences. Without consequences of some kind, they are likely to commit similar acts in the future.

Being mugged is one of the most vulnerable and confusing experiences. Most of us do not like being vulnerable in general, much less being physically and psychologically threatened. To be overpowered or outnumbered is intimidating and scary. This creates deep waves of emotion from panic and anger to confusion and fear. Why would they do this to me? How could someone dehumanize me in this way?

Crimes are often committed against people who the offender doesn't know. It is easier to dehumanize people we don't know. That is why getting to know your neighbors in the city is one of the best ways to be safe. But no matter how alert or cautious one might be, no one can guard against everything.

The common response to a mugging is for people to blame the victim. It makes it easier for us to understand the violence. It would be too scary to think that it could happen to anyone. Even when someone is not being careless, it is possible to be at the wrong place at the wrong time. Muggings can be random and we can't do anything to guarantee we will not become a victim to random violence.

There's nothing glamorous about muggings. But one thing I have learned from being involved in these kinds of situations is, even in the midst of these moments, God is present. In these situations, words fall short of the heart's anguish and questions. The only response is presence. All you can do is sit with someone in that discomforting space and allow the calming peace of God to enter. Ministry of presence in the aftermath of these moments is sacred. I have heard the Good Samaritan parable used a lot as a missionary story, but it is really a mugging story. A guy is jumped while traveling to the city. The man is beaten half dead. Caring for victims of violence and addressing emotional, physical, and psychological wounds is part of our vocation as loving neighbors. Sometimes we are the victims and sometimes it's our friends, neighbors, or even enemies. The maturity of our love is when we want healing as much for our enemies as our friends.

It's in life's tragedies and heartaches that we have the opportunity to show Christ's compassion to one another. We have the responsibility and honor to care for each other in moments of pain and trauma. People need permission to feel afraid, mad, confused. Being each other's neighbor is entering into the powerlessness and pain of being mistreated by the very ones you came to serve and love. It's a moment of understanding the suffering of Jesus. Jesus was vulnerable to the point of physical beating and torment. We like to think that love will be received and change will be painless. The cross reveals the opposite.

Love makes us vulnerable. Love takes us to places where we are vulnerable to jeering crowds, merciless mobs, aggressive and oppressive uniformed guards. But it is this very place of vulnerability and victimization that Christ demonstrates the depths of love. Jesus forgives the very ones who spit on him, mock him, beat him, and nail him into the wood.

It's just as confusing to be on the opposite side. I've had close friends mugged and I've also known youth who have been the muggers. I've stood at the police station with victims and in court with offenders. I've told victims not to be afraid to press charges if that is what they feel strongly about and I've pleaded for mercy from a judge for a youth who mugged someone to impress their friends.

The reality is, all of us are victims and perpetrators. We all need grace to change. We all need to let love sink into the places of pain. We can naively think that when we serve God nothing will happen to us. We call it faith, believing God would not allow anything bad to happen while we are doing what God has called us to. That's not the message of the Passion. The cross is about love's willingness to endure pain and suffering for the greater good of the world. Real faith is not the avoidance of negativity and problems; it is believing God can bring us through anything no matter how bad it looks on the surface. Even in the most horrific and tragic moments, we believe God can bring redemptive purposes. It's hard to have this faith unless you've endured hardship.

After Jenny's experience being held up, I suggested moving the team out of the neighborhood. She was adamantly against this. She wanted to stay in the same neighborhood where she and the team had built relationships. We moved them off the block, but they still remained in the same neighborhood. I was shocked at her faith. She didn't want to leave. She believed that God could bring them through. That faith continues to drive her. She stayed in the same community for the next few years investing in and advocating for the community. Only the grace of God can give us that kind of faith and courage.

While a small percentage of people engage in criminal activity for various reasons in city neighborhoods, clearly the vast majority are people – decent people, family oriented people, communal people – who want to see things get better. They take care of their lawns, wash their cars, watch out for each other's children, work, make sacrifices, pinch pennies, share, and look out for others. That is why even the most tragic moments have a way of bringing out humanity's best. There are simply more who choose to love than there are of those who choose to hate. There are more decent, compassionate, hopeful, and generous people than there are bigots, terrorists, gang bangers, and extorters. After Hurricane Katrina, of course you heard about the crazies who claimed it was the act of God, but so many more who devoted time and wrote checks to help with the recovery. After shootings, whether they are in Colorado suburbs or city streets, its not uncommon to see a groundswell of support for families of the grieved, generous donations, and even forgiveness for perpetrators. These responses show that though evil surfaces in all places in our world, it cannot stand up forever against the good that outnumbers, or at least overcomes it. There is unspeakable evil, injustice and violence in our world. Saying "God is in the city" doesn't deny that evil exists in the world – evil is all too present in the city – it simply reminds us that evil will yield when enough people stand up for what is good, just, and right.

Tragedy is not the final word for people of faith. Our faith helps us overcome fear. We don't have a naive optimism, but a tried and tested faith that stands despite the winds and waves that beat against it. Faith in God is not about avoiding suffering, but trusting God to bring redemption out of it.

Update: Josh Chastain

Since completing Mission Year in 2006-2007, Josh has served in ministries in Wheeling, WV and Indianapolis, IN working with the urban poor and living within the neighborhoods he serves. He has currently taken a leave of absence from the city to get a Master's Degree in Computing in Scotland, but he's still living simply, building relationships with all the neighbors he can and experiencing God's grace wherever he goes.

Update: Jenny Pitzen

Jenny currently works as a Social Worker with at-risk youth at a High School in the Philadelphia Suburbs. The lessons she learned and community she experienced in Chicago have certainly gone with her. Jenny continues to wrestle with what it means to be a good neighbor and to build Christian community in a new context. She is learning that God's grace and hope is just as needed in the suburbs as it is in the city.

Political Scandal

"The spiritual virtue of a sacrament is like light; although it passes among the impure, it is not polluted."

- Augustine of Hippo

In 2012, Chicago received the dubious distinction of being the number one city for corruption. In a report by the University of Illinois between 1976 and 2010, Chicago had 1,531 cases of public corruption.[4] That is only the public corruption cases. And only the ones that got caught! We certainly have had our share of high profile political scandals. Whether you are from Illinois or not, you have probably heard about Blago, our former Governor Rod Blagojevich. He was impeached and convicted for attempting to sell Obama's senate seat.

Mission Year had two volunteers that worked at Chicago Christian Industrial League (CCIL) where Rod's wife worked. Now, everyone knows about the scandal and everyone now knows Blago, but not many people realize the crazy work God was doing in the midst of this.

Jimmie Beck is a janitor at CCIL that our Mission Year teams have grown to love. Jimmie is an incredibly humble man of faith. He also has a record from dealing drugs in the past that has continued to haunt him and minimize his job prospects. Despite the setbacks, he always has a smile on his face and is always quick to share his testimony.

One time Steve Wilkos, Jerry Springer's old bodyguard, came to CCIL to do a show at the homeless shelter for a special Thanksgiving special. He served a meal, listened to the guys' stories, and highlighted the issues of drugs and poverty.

He brought Jimmie into his private trailer and interviewed him on national television. Jimmie told him how he used to sell drugs and served time in prison but how he had turned his life around. Steve asked, "So how did you escape a life of drugs?"

Jimmie said, "God."

Steve said, "No, really how did you do it."

Jimmie said "God."

Jimmie was always quick to stand up for God and we were about to see God stand up for Jimmie.

On the day Blago was impeached, my heart was full of gratitude. Not because of his unfortunate circumstances, but because of what he did in his final act. Here's one newspaper's account of the events:

"Only hours before the Illinois Senate unanimously removed Rod Blagojevich as Governor the disgraced politician was hard at work issuing two controversial last minute pardons. As his own fate was being debated by the Illinois Senate, Blagojevich was making important and far reaching decisions.

While it may seem inappropriate that a Governor accused of corruption still be able to issue pardons, according to legal experts it is completely in keeping the letter, if not the spirit, of Illinois law. Blagojevich pardoned two criminals on the day he was removed from office; Fred S. Latsko who was convicted of forgery and deception in 1985, and Jimmie L. Beck who had served time for drug offenses.

'It's just a blessing,' Beck said after learning of the pardon from a Tribune reporter. 'I believe it's the work of the Lord. It's hard getting employment when you got a [criminal] background.'[5]

All the media sources were scrambling to figure out who this Jimmie was. But we knew and were overjoyed at how God was able to bring about such good in the midst of such corruption. No one deserved it more than Jimmie. When we saw Jimmie the next day he said, "Some trust in chariots and some in horses, but I trust in the name of the Lord." What is most inspiring to me about the story, is that even in the midst of political scandal and corruption, God is still able to bring about good. God brings down the proud and gives grace to the humble.

Update: Rod "Blago" Blagojevich

Blagojevich has served two years of a fourteen-year sentence for corruption at FCI Englewood Prison in Littleton, Colorado. He is teaching Civil War history in prison and learning to play the guitar. His lawyer is appealing his sentence.

Update: Jimmie Beck

Jimmie L. Beck is working at A Safe Haven, formerly CCIL, a not for profit, social enterprise that helps people aspire, transform, and sustain their lives as they transition from homelessness to self-sufficiency with pride and purpose.

Principalities and Powers

"Our struggle is not against flesh and blood, but against principalities and powers."

- Ephesians 6:12

When you live in the city, especially in places of concentrated poverty and injustice, you see larger powers at work. Paul talked about our struggle not being against flesh and blood, but principalities and powers.[6] I grew up hearing that but never really knowing what principalities and powers were. Now I understand.

Jesus talks about there being an enemy that seeks to steal, kill, and destroy.[7] Principalities and powers are the systems and forces at work in the world that steal, kill, and destroy human life. Gang violence, drugs, addiction, poverty, homelessness, human trafficking, greed, exploitation, corruption, abuse, prisons, broken families – all of these steal, kill, and destroy. All of these rob people of experiencing God's abundant life. Principalities and powers reveal the true enemy. Our enemy is not the poor, the homeless, the single mom, the immigrant or even the rich, conservative or liberal; our enemies are the powers that seek to steal, kill, and destroy. Our mission, as Christ's body, is to resist these forces, to interrupt their presence in the lives of people and communities.

Jesus fought against the powers of evil on the cross. The cross became the place of spiritual victory over the power of sin, death, and evil. Colossians says, "the Father rescued us from the power of darkness and transferred us into the kingdom of his Beloved Son."[8] And "Christ disarmed the rulers and authorities making a public spectacle of them, triumphing over them on the cross."[9]

We had a team of women that came into conflict with the spiritual forces of darkness in their neighborhood. They felt led to go on a prayer walk in the neighborhood. They walked through the neighborhood stopping at random places to pray for the people that they were burdened over and the many issues that overshadowed their community. They stopped at a nearby elementary school playground and prayed.

Joanna, the team leader, couldn't pray because she couldn't keep her eyes off the gang graffiti that covered the playground. They lived in a neighborhood divided between two rival gangs. The gang symbols covered the playground where first and second graders were meant to play. It deeply disturbed her that kids would have to be exposed to gangs so young. She did not have to worry about gang graffiti on the playgrounds where she grew up so why should they have to here?

They continued their prayer walk, but Joanna couldn't stop thinking about the playground. She decided to talk with the principal of the school and see if they would let her paint over the gang symbols. The principal said "Of course, but we don't have any funds for you to do it." Joanna told the principal to not worry about that. She got some money from her home church and bought spray paint. She told the pastor of her neighborhood church what she wanted to do and the pastor sent some help. A high school senior who needed service hours to graduate stopped by the church that day and the pastor sent him over to paint the playground with them. While they were painting the playground three guys walked up to the high school senior and started beating him. They pulled his shirt over his head, grabbed a can of spray paint, and started beating him over the head repeatedly. The girls stood there stunned at the suddenness of the attack. One of the girls standing a few feet away screamed for them to stop. Eventually, they ran off leaving a bloody body.

The girls took the high school kid to LaVillita church where Pastor Victor washed him off and cared for his wounds. They found out that the high school senior was a former gang member who had decided he did not want to be part of it anymore. The gang members had orders to beat him up whenever they saw him.

Pastor Victor called a friend who does gang intervention. They set up a meeting with the leaders of the gang. They brokered a deal with the gang leaders that they accept the beating he received at the playground as his official out of the gang (typically you have to endure a 3 minute beat down to exit a gang, which is one reason it is hard for youth to get out once they are in). They agreed to the terms so he was able to break free from the gang. I talked with the girls about finishing the project of painting the playground and told them I would understand if they did not want to finish (I was not sure I wanted them to finish). They were all nervous but they insisted on finishing. I agreed on one condition; I would recruit four of the biggest guys I knew from our church's recovery program to stand guard. They had no complaints.

The high school senior wanted to finish too because he was determined to change his life. Painting over the gang symbols at the playground had become a visible symbol of his own conversion from darkness to light. A simple act of prayer and service led to confrontation with the principalities and powers of evil that led to his freedom from gang life. Pastor Victor not only cared for the young man by addressing his wounds, he interceded on his behalf until he was freed from the powers that trapped him in a life of violence.

When the girls first approached me with the idea of painting the playground I have to admit I thought to myself, "the gangs will just graffiti it again." It is easy to be cynical and hopeless in the face of injustice and evil. I see now that cynicism takes no effort, but hope takes courage. If the gangs graffiti the playground again then, we need to paint it again. And again. And again. We are in an ongoing battle against evil so we have to be ready to stand strong against the powers with faith, courage, and hope.

Update: Joanna Woodrum

After participating in Mission Year Chicago in 2007-2008, Joanna moved back to her home state of North Carolina and is currently working as an academic advisor at a local community college. She enjoys living in Raleigh and assisting her community members with the process of furthering their education while providing students with the opportunity for growth and fulfillment. Joanna also continues to work with those who are experiencing homelessness and aims to constantly further practices of community, justice, and love.

Bless those who Curse You

"Now there is a final reason I think that Jesus says, 'Love your enemies.' It is this: that love has within it a redemptive power. And there is a power there that eventually transforms individuals. "

- Martin Luther King, Jr.

Ginny, one of our Mission Year volunteers, worked in a thrift store in the Roseland neighborhood on the south side of Chicago. The thrift store is a ministry in the community offering affordable clothes, furniture, and other items at very low prices. One day Ginny was working in the store when a disgruntled woman came in. The woman appeared to have a mental illness. She asked if she could get a free coat. The store gives vouchers for free clothing but it does not include coats. Ginny told the woman this and the woman began to curse and scream all kinds of obscenities at her.

Ginny remained calm and told the woman she was sorry but that's the policy. At this the woman spit in her face and exited the store. Ginny did not respond, she simply wiped the spit off her face with her sleeve and kept working. Steve, the store supervisor, heard what happened and asked her if she needed to take a break for a few moments or go to the washroom to wash. Ginny said no she was fine.

The supervisor asked curiously, "Are you angry?"

Ginny answered "No, I'm not angry. I'm sad. I'm sad that the woman is in a situation that causes her to respond that way."

There were others in the store who observed what had happened and they chimed in. "If that was me I would have jumped over the counter and given it to that lady. I would have said something back."

They were amazed at Ginny's response. It was even more impressive since she was the youngest of our volunteers. That night at church Bible study, someone brought up the incident and they ended up talking about it the entire time.

"What would you have done?"

"What does Christ call us to do in response to being cursed out and spit on?"

It was a sacred moment. Her response to bless those that curse her became a powerful witness to the community. It is a witness for all of us. How do we respond to those that curse us to our face or talk behind our backs? Is our faith deep enough to cause us to empathize with our enemies and seek their wholeness even while they curse and spit on us?

Ginny reflected on this incident,

"After the homeless woman and the customers I was helping had left, Steve, the thrift store manager, just stared at me. I asked him what was wrong and he said, 'I just saw Christ in you.' That made me deeply uncomfortable, embarrassed even. No, I thought, that can't be true. I didn't do anything remarkable. I just did my job, I was just myself. After that day at the thrift store I tried to dismiss what Steve had said. I tried to rationalize it like he was really saying something like, 'You just did that Christian thing' or 'that was Christ-like.' But Christ in me? Christ in me? No, no, no. But a year and a half later I was asking God to show me where he was during my time in Roseland, and the Holy Spirit led me back to that moment in the thrift store. The Spirit spoke to me saying, 'You were a sacrament living out an inward state of grace.' By conforming to Christ's will and example, Christ was actually seen through me. God answered my prayer and showed me where he was in the city: God was in me. What an incredible honor, what a gift. I have never been the same."

Update: Ginny Schneider

After leaving Mission Year and her "home" in the Roseland community in Chicago, Ginny moved to southern California to begin her university adventure at the Bible Institute of LA where she is training to become a better Christ follower through her studies and her dearly beloved church and school communities. Ginny hopes to become a public high school English teacher, as she believes that the power of a good education can transform not only her student's opportunities but their souls as well. She hopes that throughout her life she can encourage human flourishing through communion with God and one another.

Chicago Crucifixion

"There is a crucified people, whose crucifixion is the product of actions in history."

- Ignacio Ellacuria

I have been reflecting on the death of Derrion Albert. Not simply because it happened in one of our Mission Year neighborhoods, but because it is happening all over the city of Chicago, all over the country. It is important to remember these events, especially after they fall out of the media cycle. We have had over forty deaths of Chicago Public School students this year, Derrion's death just happened to be captured on video for the world to see. What is the significance of the death of Derrion Albert? What can we learn as a society and nation from this tragedy? What should our response as Christians be to such violence and hatred?

One thing that has been said about urban youth that I get tired of hearing is that they do not value life. I think the real problem is that we as a society do not equally value their lives. How many youth have to die before we take action? How can we allow black and brown youth in our cities to live in conditions we would never allow for white children?

Months before Derrion's death, the State cut vital funding for programs to at-risk youth, the homeless, the disabled as well as programs aimed at preventing gang violence. While at the same time, Chicago was able to find billions of dollars for an Olympic bid. The message was clear; we value the Olympics over our youth. How are they to value their lives when we do not value their lives? Ironically, some media outlets blamed Derrion Albert's viral video with putting an end to Chicago's hope for the Olympics.[10] I haven't heard anyone calling for all that money pledged for the Olympics to be invested to address the inequalities and needs of our low-income neighborhoods or at-risk youth. Wouldn't that communicate how valuable our youth really are?

When watching the video of Derrion Albert's beating, I could not help but think of the cross. The images paralleled the gospel account of Jesus' crucifixion in striking ways. Derrion, an innocent young man, is violently beaten. There is chaos and a mob mentality egging on the violence. He is struck until he collapses. He tries to stand up but falls while the mob hits him ruthlessly with a wood plank. A group of women disciples from a nearby Christian community center pick up the body to preserve it.

The reason that it so closely parallels the cross is because the cross exposes these very cycles of human violence and injustice. We are told all our lives that Jesus died on the cross for our personal sins. What we are not told is that it's so much more than that. Jesus came to bring Good News to the poor. On the cross, Jesus entered into solidarity with the "crucified poor," exposing the violence, victimization, and dehumanization the poor suffer in our world everyday. Jesus exposes the religious hypocrisy of the religious leaders, the political corruption of the Roman leaders, and the economic exploitation of the moneychangers – the systems that perpetuate injustice. Christ died on the cross not simply to forgive us our sins, but to shake up the whole social order – to transform everything (individuals, communities, cultures, religious, political, and economic systems). The cross brings the marginalized into the center and should cause us to examine all those who are dehumanized, unjustly sentenced, and victimized by violence. Not only that, in the same way we say "it was my sin that nailed Jesus to the cross," we should reflect on how we are culpable in the suffering of the poor. Jesus was calling the church to the margins to live in solidarity with those who suffer, believing that as we witness to peace, love, and justice we will see God's kingdom come. Discipleship is "taking up our cross and following Jesus," and entering into the struggle against sin in our lives (personal righteousness) and also in the world (social justice). The cross gives us hope that the forces of evil, sin, hatred, injustice, and violence will not ultimately overcome nonviolent resistance, forgiveness, and love.

In the crucifixion story, it is not the mobs that are ultimately responsible for Jesus death, it is us. It is our collective sin that led Jesus to the cross, to bear the weight of our sin. In a similar way, the poor bear the unjust weight of the collective sin of our society. When we fail to act, neglect the poor, tolerate gross inequalities, we participate in the crucifixion of the poor. We give the order to crucify them when we ignore their plight, cut funding for life-saving programs, or when we demonize African American youth rather than respond with compassion and action. Jesus' death is trying to open our eyes to the violence that is done daily to the vulnerable, the innocent sufferers, and the poor, and to see how we share responsibility in it.

We look at the youth that committed the crimes and call them "Monsters," when we have also stood by as spectators to the crimes committed to the poor. The video of Derrion Albert is an indictment against us. It reveals our lack of action. We simply watch the video from the sidelines and pass judgment on how awful it is. But we do not advocate for major investments into the communities where violence breeds, nor do we follow the example of Jesus and give our own lives in redemptive suffering. Jesus suffered with and for the poor. Is not that the Christian response to such violence and hatred?

Arne Duncan and Eric Holder came to Roseland to interview kids at Fenger High School to figure out what the kids need. They concluded that parents need to be more involved, more funding needs to go into Saturday and afterschool programs (which had been previously cut), and youth need mentors and role models. So who is going to step up? Where are the followers of Jesus? Are we not called to lay down our lives in love for others? Are we not called to take up our cross, be willing to suffer for the sake of love?

Diane Latiker, a woman from the Roseland community, has sacrificed her life to save lives. She is tired of the killings. She erected a memorial to the fallen youth in Roseland to honor and remember their lives. In the memorial over 220 stones are displayed with names and ages of youth who died because of violence in the Roseland community since 2007 (she's behind by 150). While standing in silence in front of the memorial and reading the names of children and youth from ages 1 to 24, I could only imagine God's grief over precious lives lost, crucified in the streets of Chicago.

Diane started Kids Off the Block to interrupt the violence and offer youth an option besides hanging out on the corner. She opened her home to tutor, mentor, and provide a safe haven for youth. We need more people like Diane.

Jesus commissioned his disciples to bring good news to the poor, to give the blind new sight, and raise the dead. Death is all around us in the city. When we invest in the lives of at-risk youth, we can literally save their lives. We can prevent the precious loss of life. We can let youth know they are valued. We can make sure what happened to Derrion Albert doesn't happen again. We can raise the dead to life.

Resurrection is about hope. We raise kids from the dead when we can fill them with hope about their future and help them understand how valuable they are and share with them the same opportunities and resources as we provide our own kids. I believe this is the best way we can honor Derrion Albert.

Update: Diane Latiker

For 12 years, Diane has been in the Roseland community offering youth an alternative, an answer to the complex and perplexing problem of youth violence. Her work has even been recognized nationally as she made the top ten of CNN heroes in 2011. That same year, Diane's organization Kids Off the Block was a Mission Year service site partner.

CHAPTER TEN

IN YOUR WILDEST DREAMS
ENCOUNTERS OF HOPE AND RESURRECTION

"It is not more surprising to be born twice than once; everything in nature is resurrection."
- Voltaire

"Everything that is done in the world is done by hope."
- Martin Luther

Life comes out of death and those going through suffering often are the ones who bear witness to hope. As we enter into the suffering and death in our community, we are able to experience resurrection and hope. We find that hope is always trying to bust through the cracks. We have a future hope. Because grace is always at work, we can anticipate and expect resurrection.

In Your Wildest Dreams

"Hold fast to dreams for if dreams die,
Life is a broken-winged bird that cannot fly.
Hold fast to dreams for when dreams go,
Life is a barren field frozen with snow."

- Langston Hughes

One morning after having some good prayer time, I walked out my front door and saw a group of guys congregating on the corner across the street. Drug dealing is something I have gotten used to seeing on the block so I did what I normally do: I pretended I didn't see them and just kept walking straight to my car. But this time, I stopped myself halfway into the car. I turned around and walked over to the group of guys and started talking.

I told them about a dream I felt God had given me for our community. I told them I wanted to get people with money to invest in the dreams of people in our community. After I finished talking, they asked me if I was a politician. I said "No." I told them I live in the neighborhood, right across the street actually, and go to the church around the corner. They said they go to church too.

They said, "People think just because we sell drugs we don't believe in God."

Then one of the guys said, "Do you think we want to be doing this?"

I asked, "What would you do if you could do anything?" I guess I expected to hear him say be a rapper or professional athlete, but what he said surprised me.

He said, "I've always thought about starting a youth center over there by that empty lot. There aren't many places for youth to go."

This sparked something in the next guy who said, "I've always wanted to start my own business and hire shorties from the neighborhood since there aren't many jobs here."

Pretty incredible dreams. I left feeling joy and sadness at the same time. Joy about having such an open conversation with guys on the block and sadness with the reality that I live in a neighborhood where dreams die.

Dreams are sacred. Dreams allow every one of us to imagine what life could be, what we could be. Dreams stir up hope. In the gospel of Luke, Mary sings a song of expectation about the coming Savior. "He has brought down rulers from their thrones, but has lifted up the humble. He has filled the hungry with good things, but sent away the rich empty."[1] She believes the child she bears will usher in a different kind of kingdom where the humble, humiliated, and poor are given a place of prominence. Christ gives hope to those left out of the systems of power. They are dared to dream.

Living in the city, I have realized that some of us have the privilege of being able to pursue our dreams while others see their dreams die. We live in a world where you need to know the right people or have enough money to follow your dream.

What about those that can't afford to go to college to pursue their passion?

What about those that cannot get conventional loans to start small businesses?

What about the guys on the block who have dreams but can't see a way to make them reality?

Does God only give dreams to the wealthy and well-connected? Is dreaming only for the privileged?

I believe God is a dreamer. Part of the divine image we all bear is that we are dreamers too. Believing and investing in the dreams of others, especially those living in communities where dreams die, is a holy undertaking. That is why Mission Year invests so much time and resources into the neighborhoods we serve.

Dreams are not reserved for the rich alone. Christ has come to awaken the hopes and dreams of the poor. Drug dealers dream too.

New Creations

"Beauty awakens the soul to act."
- Dante Alighieri

One of the homeless shelters in the Lawndale neighborhood decided to create a large mural on the side of their building. The shelter was a brand new building with state of the art services including medical, job training, food pantry, and support services. The only problem was, no one in the community knew they were there. They wanted residents to know about their services and to feel comfortable coming in and hoped the mural would raise awareness. They contacted a local mural artist to do a mural on their outside wall. Before they do anything, they meet with community members and ask about what events have defined the community, what struggles still exist, and what images provoke inspiration and hope.

After getting feedback from people, they created a design. Some of our Mission Year volunteers were involved in the project so we were able to witness the transformation of this blank brick wall into a work of art. First, they gathered broken glass, bottles, and found objects on the streets surrounding the shelter. They took the broken glass and separated it into different colors and then used the broken glass to create different images on the mural. The finished product was beautiful and inspiring. A father lifting up his son in the air, kid's playing, a woman holding a boutique of flowers, the neighborhood's historic greystone houses along with some of the services the organization provided. The wall was transformed from a blank wall into a beautiful portrait of the neighborhood's story.

The muralist in charge of the project had this to say about the importance of public art:

"Imagine a world without public art. Remove from our libraries the kinds of paintings and sculptures that you find inside there. Strip all that out. What do you have left? Essentially sidewalks, streets, parking meters, signs. Some very nice parks. But by stripping out all the art, you end up dehumanizing things. Public art has the ability to express aspirations and contradictions. It has the ability to challenge people in unexpected ways. It has the ability to cause us to laugh. [Public art gives people] a sense of history, place, location, a sense of belonging that you would not have otherwise if your environment was made out of advertising signs and directional signs. Public art allows us to reflect on greater intellectual, aesthetic, spiritual and community values with more complexity than we would have otherwise."[2]

Art gives us creative eyes to see possibility where others see debris. Instead of staring at the sides of plain, brick buildings, residents see potential and possibilities. Possibility is what creates hope and hope creates change. Art and murals reflect what is good in creation, and also point to new creation. Simply seeing the old creation can lead to despair and hopelessness. Murals infiltrate our doubts and inflate our dreams. We see new creations in the midst of the old. We see how all the broken fragments of our neighborhood will one day be restored into beautiful works of art.

Green My Hood

"We have lived our lives by the assumption that what was good for us would be good for the world. We have been wrong. We must change our lives so that it will be possible to live by the contrary assumption, that what is good for the world will be good for us. And that requires that we make the effort to know the world and learn what is good for it."

- Wendell Berry

Leroy Barber, friend and former President of Mission Year, is a visionary and a force for God's kingdom. He is always thinking of new ways to build community or expand God's kingdom through partnership and innovation. After reading a book on environmental racism, he was convicted to start a new initiative called "Green my Hood." Green my Hood is about bringing the environmental movement to the streets where Leroy lives and other urban neighborhoods across the country. Since urban neighborhoods are hit hardest by environmental pollution, greening the hood is a way we love our neighbors and a way to organize the community to take action.

Greening our hoods is simple. It can mean starting a community garden, picking up trash, taking energy efficient light bulbs to neighbors, starting recycling programs, creating murals to inspire creativity and change, taking public transportation, or planting trees and flowers. These simple practices increase the quality of life for the entire neighborhood.

Making our neighborhoods greener makes them safer. When people see a neighborhood that is green it reduces criminal behavior. In an article in *The Atlantic*, Emily Badger shares the results of a study by University of Pennsylvania researchers on a 10-year project in

Philadelphia to convert vacant lots into park space.[3] They found that gun-related violence significantly declined in areas around the lots that had been greened. Vandalism and criminal behavior were also reduced. They also found that residents in some areas around these newly converted green spaces reported feeling less stress and getting more exercise.

Charles C. Branas, associate professor of epidemiology who led the research concluded:

"With respect to safety, both the broken windows and incivilities theories support our findings, and we can speculate that violent crime may have simply been discouraged in the presence of greened and tended vacant lots which signaled that someone in the community cared and was potentially watching over the space in question."

The focus of Green My Hood is not simply environmentalism. We green our hoods because we care about our communities. Creation care is community care. Simple acts help others take notice. One time we were doing a trash pickup with youth from our neighborhood. They were picking up bottles and trash in empty lots and in the alleys. One guy walked by and almost dropped his wrapper on the ground but then he saw the youth. He made his way over to the trash can instead and threw it out. Sometimes it seems like an uphill battle, but every act is significant and makes a statement of how we want our neighborhood to be. It begins with education. I first made the connection between caring for creation and my faith in seminary when my seminary professor Howard

Synder told the class, "Recycling is a discipleship issue." Through Green My Hood and many other local initiatives, kids are learning much earlier the vital importance of taking care of our planet.

Green My Hood is also an opportunity to highlight structural issues of environmental racism and injustice. Nationwide, 60 percent of African Americans and Latinos live in communities with uncontrolled toxic waste sites.[4] In Houston, Texas – where black males make up slightly more than one quarter of the local population—more than 75 percent of the municipal garbage incinerators and 100 percent of the city-owned garbage dumps are located in black neighborhoods.[5] According to a 2004 study by the League of United Latin American Citizens, 7 in 10 Hispanics live in counties that violate air pollution standards.[6]

Thankfully, there are organizations that are targeting the larger structural issues affecting communities. Some issues require collective action and political advocacy. One environmental organization has been fighting to close down a coal plant in our neighboring community that has been linked to causing brain damage and asthma in residents. After ten years of organizing and lobbying by concerned residents and community activists, it is finally being closed down. Others have been advocating for recycle bins in low-income communities like they have in wealthier areas of our city. After many years, our neighborhood finally has them.

Celebrating Green My Hood Day is simple: set aside the last Saturday in May to value and beautify your community. Even better, organize a group of friends to do it with you (#greenmyhood). Last year there were volunteers all over the country that took part in greening their hoods. Greening our hoods take individual and collective action. A green hood means a safer, cleaner, and healthier hood for everyone.

Update: Leroy Barber

Leroy Barber is the Global Executive Director for Word Made Flesh, an international community serving Jesus among the most vulnerable of the world's poor, and serves on the boards of the Christian Community Development Association and The Simple Way. He is a national speaker and author of *"Red, Brown, Yellow, Black and White: Who's More Precious In God's Sight?"* Leroy lives in Portland with his wife Donna.

Don't Quit Church

"Faith is the bird that sings when the dawn is still dark."
- Rabindranath Tagore

Have you ever wanted to quit church? If so, you are not alone. I know countless others that have struggled with church or been burned by so-called Christians. Before going to Chicago, I had a bad church experience that made me wonder if I should just quit church altogether. I questioned whether the church had any relevance for the rest of the world. I almost gave up hope. I decided I would give the urban church one last chance. I'm glad I did.

It has been refreshing to go to a church that is focused on the community. I attend Lawndale Community Church. Our church has a health clinic that employs over 400 people, a sit down restaurant because there aren't any in the neighborhood, a recovery home for men, community development corporation that provides affordable houses and apartments, jobs for life program, and kids and youth ministries. The church is outward focused and it has made an impact that is visible.

Our church has a casual feel. When it started they wanted to make sure anybody could come as they are and be accepted as they are. So some people dress casual while others like dressing up. Services are not polished. You won't see fancy lighting or jumbo trans. The church has a simple focus on loving God, loving people.

I have come to really appreciate African American spirituality too. Lee Butler, a professor of African American spirituality at Chicago Theological Seminary, says the main mode of European

Christianity is the mind, while the main mode of African American Spirituality is the emotions. Entering into African American Christianity has helped me to engage my emotions as well as my mind. Many European churches are afraid of emotionalism, but we probably should be more afraid of emotionless Christianity. The church is not dying from too much emotion! Our emotions are as sacred as our thoughts. Our mind and emotions are both ways we have been made in God's image. To deny our emotions is to deny part of who God created us to be.

Feeling emotions, the full range, is a gift the city provides. Never have I felt such agony and ecstasy, sorrow and joy. Church has helped me feel both. We suffer together when one of our members can't find a job, when one of our brothers falls back into drugs, or when a precious young life is taken too soon. Likewise, we celebrate together when one of our members comes home from the hospital after battling a health condition, when a couple in our church gets married, and when one of our youth heads off to college.

Church is also a place that sets us free. Historically, the black church has been a place of liberation. Church was the place where blacks could be free, even if temporarily, from the racism and oppression of slavery and Jim Crow. Worship is about liberation. Dancing, clapping, and singing helps us free our souls even though our bodies may be chained and our world still in bondage.

Church is where tired souls find strength from each other, where truth and hope bolster us in times of discouragement and despair. Ms. Pam, a neighbor, seasoned youth minister, and mentor for so many of us younger do-gooders, sings a song every once and awhile in church that has a powerful effect on the entire congregation. The song is called "I'm not tired yet." The words are: "I've been running with Jesus a long time, I'm not tired yet. I've been working for Jesus a mighty long time. I'm not tired yet. No! I'm not tired yet. No! I'm not tired yet." It keeps repeating and Ms. Pam sings it with conviction and passion.

Sometimes it seems like she is singing it to convince herself to keep going, but mostly I believe she is trying to convince us. If she is not quitting after many years and battles, then we better not even think about it. When people are moved by a solo during the Sunday morning service they stand up. You might see four or five people standing during a typical solo. By the time Ms. Pam is finished, just about everybody is up on their feet. Her singing and her life are testaments of perseverance, a righteous refusal to quit or accept tiredness when so much is still left to be done. Ms. Pam reflects what church is at its best: hope in struggle, and fuel for the ongoing battle against despair, evil, and injustice.

Update: Pam McCain

Ms. Pam is a children's ministry leader at Lawndale Community Church and a Middle School Teacher at Daystar School. She lives in North Lawndale with her husband where she inspires many through her deep faith and love of children.

Future

"To be what we are, and to become what we are capable of becoming, is the only end of life."

- Robert Louis Stevenson

Daniel was a volunteer who came to Chicago to do Mission Year right out of high school. During his year of service he lived and went to church in LaVillita, a Latino neighborhood on the west side of Chicago. He was involved at his church and he would go with members of the church to do outreach to day laborers who waited for work outside of Home Depot. The church would provide food and build relationships with the guys. They would also invite them to church where they could find community and other resources.

One day, he saw a younger guy there and they struck up a conversation in Daniel's limited Spanish and the young man's limited English. The young man wanted to learn English and asked if Daniel could meet with him. Daniel wanted to improve his Spanish so he said yes, and they set up a time to meet at Daniel's church. When they met up, they realized they had not exchanged names.

Daniel told the young man, "My name is Daniel."

The young man said, "My name is Daniel too."

Then they asked each other's age. English speaking Daniel said, "I am 19."

Spanish speaking Daniel said, "I am 19."

Surprised by these coincidences, they continued talking. Things were going along well until English Speaking Daniel said a word that the other Daniel could not understand. Try as he may, Daniel could not get Spanish speaking Daniel to understand.

The word was "become," as in, "Who do you want to become?"

Daniel's story of growing up in a middle class family in Michigan was very different from the other Daniel's story of immigrating to the United States from Mexico in order to get a job to make money for his family back home. He realized he had privileges the other Daniel did not. He realized that he could just have easily been born in the other Daniel's shoes and that shouldn't limit someone's opportunities or future. He realized some people have the opportunity to have a future, to think about the future, and to plan a future while others do not.

Many youth in communities like ours have no sense of future. When you don't have a future, you are always living in the present. Some youth in our neighborhood do not believe they will live past 20. If you do not believe you have a future, why save money, stay in school, or think about who you will become?

To have a future means you have a destination, a goal, and a direction that gives you purpose and trajectory for your life. Without a future there is no hope. The Jewish people in Jeremiah's time could not see a future for themselves. They had been captured and taken as exiles to Babylon. In the midst of their hopelessness, Jeremiah speaks this prophetic word over the people, "'for I know the plans I have for you,' declares the LORD, 'plans to prosper you and to give you hope and a future.'"[7]

God is in the business of giving a future to those that can't see one. Like Daniel, I never realized what a grace a future is. Having witnessed the ways many ministries are giving youth a future, I am even more convinced that the church needs to be in the future business. We have to help children and youth do more than survive the mean streets today, we need to help them learn to become.

Daniel (Mission Year volunteer)

Since Mission Year, God has broken Daniel's heart for the nations and sharing the gospel in the 10/40 window. He is now a missionary full-time working on films geared to show the power of Christ's love in the cultural context of the people and share with them the hope of an eternal future with the creator of the universe after this life.

Becoming a King

"As we move into the 21st century, it's going to be incumbent upon all of us to realize that while Martin Luther King Jr. was a great and awesome man, that we too have a calling and assignment in this life."

- Bernice A. King

I love Dr. Martin Luther King, Jr. He is a hero of mine and someone that I admire and seek to exemplify. His life and message of nonviolence, love and justice have captivated my life. His book *Strength to Love* really steered my heart to the path of faith and justice in my early days in Chicago. I would like to be like him in just about every way.

On the Sunday morning that I stood in church to testify to the grace I felt welling up inside me, I was really feeling the spirit move. It was Martin Luther King Sunday and I couldn't contain the grace and joy I was experiencing. In a moment of passion I said, "I want to be a white Martin Luther King." I heard some laughter. Some clapping. Some "Amens." Others had some confused looks on their faces wondering what that meant. I'm not even sure I knew what I meant. All I knew was that I felt so compelled by the vision and life of King, that I wanted my whole life to be directed and focused towards love and justice. In that moment, I felt a grace calling me to follow in the way of justice whatever it might cost.

Nine years later, one of the deacons in the church still calls me "Dr. King" every time he sees me. For the longest time I was embarrassed when he said it. I didn't want him to think I thought so highly of myself that I would compare myself to Martin Luther King. But now I know why he does it. One, because he likes me. You get a nickname because you are liked. Two, every time he says it he is causing me to remember that Sunday. He is letting me know he remembers that Sunday and what God did in me. He was a witness to my transformation and is helping me not forget. We need people in our lives to remind us who we want to become.

This past January, I found out Elder Bernice A. King, one of Dr. King's daughters, was scheduled to preach at a church on the south side. I jumped at the opportunity to hear her. I arrived at the church and the ushers squeezed me into a seat between two older African American ladies. I sat with anticipation to hear the word she prepared to speak. I felt pretty overwhelmed with the challenges of urban life and the enormous injustices we face. Elder King spoke about peace. To have peace in the world we have to have peace in God. She talked about the church's vocation of peace in the world.

She mentioned a few things that surprised me. She said she doesn't like using the phrase "civil rights movement." She said Dr. King was a prophet and that it was a Holy Spirit movement, a God movement. As we submit our lives to God, our lives can become channels of God's peace to the world.

She talked about when their home was bombed because they refused to move out of Alabama. They received death threats on a regular basis. She said her mom, Coretta, was just as courageous in the face of the violence as her father. She was at home with her mother when their home was bombed. Coretta's parents urged her to leave and come stay with them. Coretta refused to leave and decided to stay with Martin. Bernice said, "Only the peace of God can allow someone to make that decision." Later that night, a large group of King's supporters came to the house ready to retaliate for the bombing. Dr. King talked about the importance of nonviolence and not responding to violence with violence. Again Bernice repeated, "Only the peace of God can cause people to respond to that kind of violence with peace." She urged us as we face the violence in our communities and work to end it to make sure we have peace with God. It is our connection to God that allows us to be witnesses of peace in the world.

Before she even finished preaching, I was opening my heart to receive grace from God. She told us about a defining moment in King's life. King came to point of crisis and decision. He had to decide if he would continue in the struggle or back away. "My friends and associates are being arrested. It would be the height of cowardice for me to stay away. I would rather be in jail ten years than desert my people now. I have begun the struggle, and I can't turn back. I have reached the point of no return." King had come to a decisive point of commitment to the cause.

She made an altar call for those that feel they are passed the point of no return in the fight for justice and peace. I immediately went up. I joined a group of others around the altar. I wanted to solidify this call to be a witness of God's justice and peace.

Then she talked about her name: Bernice A. King. Her initials are B. A. King. She said it's a reminder to her to "be a King." Not only to uphold the tradition of her family name, but to be a child of the King. Scripture says we are "a royal priesthood,"[8] "heirs of

God,"[9] and that "if we suffer with Christ, we will reign with Christ."[10] If we enter into the suffering of Christ and the crucified poor, we will share in the resurrection of Christ in glory. We will be Kings. She gave us a blessing and exhortation to "be a King" and live as royal ambassadors of God's kingdom in the world. She challenged us to be kings who raise the standard and live selflessly for others. In her prayer, she passed onto us the mantle she had received as the daughter of Dr. King and as a daughter of Christ the King. It was a powerful moment of grace. Tears streamed down my eyes. After the prayer, I turned and hugged the people around me and left the church with a new sense of vision and determination.

I had passed the point of no return.

As I drove home, it hit me what had really happened in that divine moment.

I had become a King.

EPILOGUE

God is in the City is a tribute to the neighborhoods and the people that have been part of my own transformation. I like to think I was part of theirs too. We have been transformed together. As we are transformed, we become part of God's larger movement of hope and change in the city. This is when our lives, like the city, become sacraments of grace for others. Our transformation is not meant for us alone, but to be shared with the rest of the world, including our families, communities, churches, governments, economic systems, school systems, and our environment.

This book focuses on how God is in the city, but God is not just in Chicago or other major urban areas. God is in every city because God is everywhere. God is in the slums and the suburbs, the White House and the crack house. God is all around us and in every moment. Most importantly, God is in us.

At the end of the day, we don't save anyone or fix anything. That's God's work. We are simply witnesses of grace who pray, speak up, and act for justice. I will never be able to repay the grace I have been given. All I can do is devote the rest of my life to sharing the grace I have freely received, build beloved community across all dividing lines, and work for justice and peace. Let us all continue to sow seeds of grace liberally, knowing that through our failures and successes the kingdom of God will continue to come.

ACKNOWLEDGEMENTS

I first want to express my thanks to God for drawing me to the city. I am thankful for all the graces God has bestowed in my life and in my time in Chicago.

I want to thank my wife for being my partner and responding to the call to the city together. I love our lives together.

I want to thank the communities of East Garfield Park, North Lawndale, La Villita, Englewood, and Roseland in Chicago, and all the other communities that have welcomed Mission Year teams and shown us so much about grace and love.

I want to thank the local leaders, mentors, pastors, and prophets who refuse to lose faith. Your hope in struggle is inspirational to many.

I want to thank my editing team (Emily Arvizu, Ashleigh Hill, and Jennifer Casselberry) for your many contributions to this book.

I want to thank all the Mission Year alumni who have opened themselves to the grace of the city and were willing to share their stories.

I want to thank our Mission Year staff, supporters and board who believe in the work of Mission Year and sustain our work in neighborhoods across the country.

Lastly, I want to thank you for reading these stories. I hope you have encountered grace in these pages and I hope you will continue to look for grace in your own city.

Questions for Personal Reflection and Group Discussion

Introduction: Developing Eyes to See

1. How do you see the city? How do you see God?

2. Do you have trouble seeing God in the city? Why or why not?

3. Where do you see grace and hope breaking through in your life and in your city? Where have you encountered God in the city?

Chapter 1: Encounters of Grace and Love

1. Have you had an experience of being baptized into a community? What did it feel like?

2. Who do you consider your family? How have they shown you grace? How have you experienced grace from others?

3. Does guilt keep you from receiving grace from others, God, yourself?

4. Have you fallen in love with your city? What's your story?

5. Are you a grateful person or do you struggle showing gratitude?

6. Have you ever been approached by a beggar? How did you feel? How did you respond? How do you think God would respond? What does the encounter with the beggar reveal about you?

7. What are the limits of your grace? Who do you struggle loving? How are you being challenged to go beyond the limits of your grace?

Chapter 2: Encounters of Humility and Wisdom

1. What does Foots' story cause you to feel? What does it lead you to do?

2. Do you have a mentor? Are there indigenous, local leaders you can place yourself under to learn from?

3. What do you think it means to have childlike faith? What have you learned from children in your life about how to enter into the kingdom?

4. Have you experienced a rite of passage? Do you have rites of passage for young people in your life?

Chapter 3: Encounters of Brokenness and Wholeness

1. Have you ever struggled with an addiction of any kind? How have you sought and/or experienced freedom? Are you helping others find freedom in that area?

2. Where has God been shining light on your cracks?

3. Have you ever been to counseling? Why or why not?

4. How would you name your sickness? What is the cure?

Chapter 4: Encounters of Rest and Remembrance

1. Do you struggle taking a Sabbath? What's the purpose of Sabbath for you?

2. Is it possible for you to find solitude without leaving the city?

3. Scripture says, "Remember those in prison as if you yourself were in chains." How do you remember those in prison?

Chapter 5: Encounters of Peace and Reconciliation

1. What does communion mean to you?

2. Are you a relational bridge? What communities are you bridging? What challenges do you face?

3. What are you willing to sacrifice for reconciliation?

4. How do you respond to conflict? How are you being led to witness for peace in your community?

5. What are the struggles in your history? How are they similar or different from the struggles of others you know?

Chapter 6: Encounters of Community and Service

1. Who is your community? What has been your most authentic experience of community?

2. Do you know your neighbors? What are ways you can be a neighbor to those on your block or those in need?

3. Have you ever received unexpected hospitality from someone? What was it like?

4. Have you ever encountered Christ in the face of the poor, stranger, widow, or orphan?

Chapter 7: Encounters of Protest and Resistance

1. Have you ever been to a march or protest? What was it like?

2. What makes you angry? What do you want to see change?

3. What things cause you to stand up and speak out?

Chapter 8: Encounters of Justice and Generosity

1. Have you ever been in a courtroom? What was your experience like?

2. What do you think the difference is between human justice and God's justice?

3. Is justice blind? Have you ever witnessed justice being done?

4. What have you learned about justice through your encounters?

5. Have you ever seen God multiply resources through sharing?

Chapter 9: Encounters of Lament and Suffering

1. What do you lament?

2. Have you ever been the victim of a break in or mugging?

3. What is your experience with the cops?

4. What principalities and powers do you see at work in your community that are stealing, killing, and destroying life?

5. Have you ever blessed someone who cursed you?

6. How do you embrace the cross in your daily life?

Chapter 10: Encounters of Resurrection and Hope

1. How has your experience with art given you hope?

2. What are ways you would like to Green Your Hood?

3. Who do you want to become? What kind of future do you see for yourself? How do you see yourself helping others envision a future for themselves?

4. Have you passed the point of no return in the struggle for justice and peace?

ORGANIZATIONS FEATURED IN THIS BOOK

Alterna Community

Alterna is an experiment in Christian missional living, welcoming the stranger and offering hospitality to Jesus who often visits us as an unauthorized immigrant from Latin America.

www.alternacommunity.com

Bethel New Life, Inc.

Bethel New Life is a 501c3 non-profit organization based in Chicago, Illinois. Formed by a small Lutheran church on the West Side of Chicago in response to the devastation and disinvestment that followed the civil rights riots of the late 1960s, Bethel New Life has been in the business of creating social impact and community change for more than three decades. To realize God's vision of a restored society by creating opportunities for individuals and families to invest in themselves and by promoting policies and systems that help communities thrive.

www.bethelnewlife.org

Breakthrough Urban Ministries

Breakthrough demonstrates the compassion of Christ by partnering with those affected by poverty to build connections, develop skills and open doors of opportunity.

www.breakthrough.org.

Christian Community Development Association

CCDA's mission is to inspire, train, and connect Christians who seek to bear witness to the Kingdom of God by reclaiming and restoring under-resourced communities.

www.ccda.org.

Celestial Ministries Drumline

Celestial Ministries exists to enhance the development of young leaders by using the word of God, music and the arts to inspire and mentor children of the incarcerated and other disadvantaged children in North Lawndale/Englewood communities.

www.celestialmin.org

Faith Community of Saint Sabina's

The Faith Community of St. Sabina is a Word-based, Bible teaching church that believes in the power of praise and worship. Our purpose is to nurture and develop spiritually mature Christians who are trained leaders and who are not confined by the walls of the sanctuary, but can penetrate the world in order to present God's way of living as a divine option.

www.saintsabina.org

Kids off the Block

Kids off the Block, Inc (KOB) is a non-profit corporation founded by Diane Latiker in 2003. KOB is a multi-service youth program that, within a holistic framework, focuses on all aspects of young peoples lives: health, education, achievement, personal and social growth.

www.kobchicago.org

Lawndale Community Church

Lawndale Community Church is a nondenominational Christian Church that seeks to provide a place to worship Jesus Christ. We place importance on a personal relationship with God through His Son Jesus Christ and growth in Him through the meeting both the spiritual and physical needs of the community through involvement in people's lives.

www.lawndalechurch.org

LaVillita Community Church

We, La Villita Community Church, as part of the body of Christ, exist in fellowship to love and glorify God by worshiping him, knowing him and making him known. Nosotros, La Villita Community Church, como parte del cuerpo de Cristo, existimos en comunion para amar y glorificar a Dios, adorándole, conociéndole y dándolo a conocer.

www.lavillitacommunitychurch.com

Love Without Agenda

Love Without Agenda is a non-profit network of social innovators catalyzing doing good in our local and global communities.

www.lovewithoutagenda.com

Mission Year

Mission Year is a national Christian ministry committed to love God, love people, and work for justice in the city. Mission Year is an entry point into a lifestyle of faith, community, service, and justice that provides young adults with the opportunity to become part of the life of an urban neighborhood in Atlanta, Chicago, Houston, and Philadelphia.

www.missionyear.org

Roseland Christian Ministries

Roseland Christian Ministries is a ministry committed to serving God and God's people in the Roseland community in Chicago. We serve God and God's people through a variety of ministries including our Strong Tower Interim Housing, After School and Summer Youth Programs, Homes Renewal Program, as well as various other ministries that flow from the worshipping congregation of Roseland Christian Ministries- Roseland Christian Reformed Church.

www.roselandchristianministries.org

Urban Mentors Network

We are passionate about mentoring, networking, building up positive community. We believe that youth need positive adults to walk alongside them for the long haul. We also believe that the strongest leaders are homegrown so we strive to involve both our youth and parents in all aspects of the Urban Mentors Network.

www.urbanmentors.com

Voices for Creative Nonviolence

Voices for Creative Nonviolence has deep, long-standing roots in active nonviolent resistance to U.S. war-making. Begun in the summer of 2005, Voices draws upon the experiences of those who challenged the brutal economic sanctions imposed by the U.S. and U.N. against the Iraqi people between 1990 and 2003.

www.vcnv.org

Young Men's Empowerment Network (YMEN)

YMEN'S mission is to prepare young men in North Lawndale for leadership by helping youth grow in their faith and character, develop love for learning, and use their talents to serve the broader community.

www.ymenchicago.com

NOTES

Introduction

[1] Stefano Esposito, "Chicago tops nation for segregation, but sees 2nd-largest decline in U.S. Report on segregation," Chicago Sun Times, January 31, 2012.
[2] When I use the word sacrament in reference to the city, I am thinking of the Anglican Book of common prayer definition of sacrament as "a visible sign of an invisible grace." The city is a sacrament because it is a physical reality capable of revealing God's invisible grace to us. In the Catholic tradition, there are seven Sacraments considered holy rituals of the Church. I am not implying the city sacraments I witness in the city are on the same level as the Eucharist or baptism. I use a lower case "s" when talking about sacraments in the city, rather than an uppercase "S" in order to make a distinction between the sacraments I observe in the city and the traditional, historic Sacraments of the Church.
[3] Genesis 28:16

Chapter One

[1] Julie Deardorff, "How extreme heat attacks the body," Chicago Tribune, July 20, 2011.
[2] Frederick Buechner, *Wishful Thinking: A Theological ABC*, (Harper & Row, 1st edition, 1973).
[3] Matthew 23:37; Luke 13:34
[4] Clay first published this story in his Mission Year support letter. It was reprinted here: Leroy Barber, *Everyday Missions*, (Downers Grove, IL: InterVarsity Press, 2012), 92-104.
[5] Proverbs 17:5; Proverbs 19:17 NLT
[6] Henri Nouwen, *Gracias! A Latin American Journal*, (Orbis Books, 1993).
[7] Revelation 21:2

Chapter Two

[1] To see photos of where the homeless sleep under Lower Wacker Dr: C. Jines, "Homeless City, Lower Wacker," Chicago Photo Journal, December 11, 2012. The city has been gradually pushing the homeless out of downtown: Cindi Richards and Diane Struzzi, "Lower Wacker to Shut Its Gates On Homeless: Fences To Be Locked, Opponents Plan Vigil," Chicago Tribune, January 29, 1999. Some of the homeless that once lived under Lower Wacker are going to other neighborhoods

like Uptown: Mark Brown, "Lower Wacker Homeless Coming to Uptown," Uptown Update, September 19, 2007. A more recent action taken against homeless: Darryl Holliday, "Anti-Homeless Barriers With Slanted Tops Installed Under Kennedy Exp," Chicago Coalition for the Homeless, May 23, 2014

[2] Teju Coles, "The White-Saviour Industrial Complex," The Atlantic, March 21, 2012.

[3] Matthew 18:3; Luke 18:17

[4] The story ends with these alienated youth mugging a couple in Central Park. He writes this as a tragic story but he means it as a wake-up call. The youth that we neglect and alienate today, become the adults that we fear tomorrow. We do not want to get mugged but we are unwilling to invest in youth so they can choose another way. Their alienation has negative consequences for them and society. Wright seems to be saying, if we won't intervene in the lives of youth because we care about them and the pain they are experiencing, at least do it for our own sake.

[5] Cynthia Dizikes, "Cook County must reform juvenile justice, national agency says: report urges demolition of temporary detention center and assails high rate of black detainees," Chicago Tribune, March 9, 2012.

[6] For a full list of the 40 Developmental Assets visit the Search Institute's website at: www.search-institute.org.

[7] Report by North Lawndale community organizer Valerie F. Leonard, "North Lawndale Education at a Glance," Policy On the Ground, May 10, 2010.

[8] Jonathan Kozol, *Savage Inequalities*, (New York: Crown, 1991), 57.

[9] Noreen S. Ahmed-Ullah, John Chase, and Bob Secter, "CPS approves largest school closure in Chicago's history," Chicago Tribune, May 23, 2013..

[10] The success of Providence St. Mel's academic achievements can be seen in the 2009 documentary called *The Providence Effect*.

Chapter Three

[1] Thomas Merton (1915-1968) is one of the most influential Catholic writers of the twentieth century. Merton was a Trappist monk, poet, social activist and writer. Merton's autobiography, *The Seven Storey Mountain*, sold millions of copies. Merton was a strong supporter of the civil rights movement and according to Daniel Berrigan, was the "conscience of the peace movement in the 1960s." Merton's life and writings exemplify the contemplative in action.

[2] 2 Corinthians 4:7 NASB

[3] John 14:26

[4] John 16:13

[5] John 8:32
[6] Matthew 13
[7] 2 Corinthians 12:9

Chapter Four

[1] Based on a 2002 study by the Center for Impact Research.
[2] Michelle Alexander, *The New Jim Crow: Mass Incarceration in the Age of Colorblindness*, (The New Press: 2012).
[3] Hebrews 13:3
[4] Matthew 25:36
[5] Isaiah 61:1; Luke 4:18
[6] For more info on Angel Tree go to: www.prisonfellowship.org/angeltree
[7] To join with others who are advocating for restorative justice and an end to mass incarceration check out: Prison Fellowship, Samuel DeWitt Proctor Conference, Change.org, The Sentencing Project, The Micah Project, Sojourners, and The Christian Community Development Association.
[8] Thomas Merton, *Conjectures of a Guilty Bystander*, (Doubleday: 1966), 81. Although this quote is often credited to Merton, he is actually quoting Douglas Steere.
[9] Julia S. Bachrach, *The City in a Garden: A History of Chicago's Parks, (Center for American Places: 2012).* This is a book of photography about Chicago's remarkable park system.
[10] Revelation 22:1-6, 12-20.
[11] The prayer is attributed to Oscar Romero but was actually written by Bishop Ken Untener of Saginaw, drafted for a homily by Cardinal John Dearden in Nov. 1979 for a celebration of departed priests. Archbishop Oscar Romero served the people of El Salvador and was assassinated in 1980 while he was saying mass in San Salvador.
[12] Malcolm Gladwell, *The Tipping Point*, (Back Bay Books, 2002),163-166.

Chapter Five

[1] Jeremy Gorner, "Chicago marks 500 homicides, City's top cop deplores gang violence, number of guns on streets, but also points out drop in overall crime," Chicago Tribune, Jan 13, 2013.
[2] William Harms, "Study: Chicago counseling program reduces youth violence, improves school engagement: Randomized trial estimates program's benefits 3 to 31 times the cost," UChicago News, July 13,

2012.

[3] Matthew 5:9

[4] Ron Magers, "Students stop violence using Philosophies of Dr. Martin Luther King, Jr.," *ABC News*, October 3, 2012.

[5] Galatians 3:28

[6] Gilbert Bilezikian, *Community 101*, (Zondervan, 1997).

Chapter Six

[1] Taken from Ron Sider, *Scandal of the Evangelical Conscience*, (Baker Books, 2005).

[2] Exodus 22:21 NLT

[3] Matthew 25:35

[4] Matthew 22:39; Mark 12:31

[5] The Parable of the Good Samaritan can be found in Luke 10:25-37.

[6] Fernando, Mejia, "Rural and Small Towns Calling for Immigration Reform Now," Alliance For a Just Society, June 10, 2014.

[7] Skid Row is the nickname for the block Elsa's team lived on in the Roseland community on the south side of Chicago.

[8] Matthew 20:26

Chapter Seven

[1] Frank James, "Martin Luther King Jr. in Chicago," Chicago Tribune Archives, August 5, 1966.

[2] The LA Times did a story on this: Richard Fausset, "Could he be a good American?," LA Times, June 4, 2011. Check out Emily Guzman's speech at the Steward Detention Center Vigil on YouTube: "American wife of immigrant detainee speaks at Stewart Detention Center Vigil IV."

[3] Micah 2:2, 9

[4] Micah 3:9-11

[5] Micah 3:11

[6] Micah 3:1-4 NLT

[7] Isaiah 1:17

Chapter Eight

[1] Psalm 147:3; Isaiah 61:1; Luke 4:18

[2] The Innocence Project reports that about 30% of DNA exoneration cases, innocent defendants made incriminating statements, delivered outright confessions or pled guilty. A variety of factors contribute to false confessions during police interrogation including: duress, coercion, intoxication, diminished capacity, mental impairment,

ignorance of the law, fear of violence, the actual infliction of harm, the threat of a harsh sentence, and misunderstanding of the situation. For more information visit the Innocence Project at: www.innocenceproject.org.

Chapter Nine

[1] Matthew 2:13-23
[2] Matthew 27:45-46
[3] Matthew 6:19
[4] "Chicago Called Most Corrupt City In Nation," CBS Chicago News, February 15, 2012.
[5] Gary Marx, "As his time in office dwindles, Blagojevich expunges criminal records of former drug dealer and real estate mogul," Chicago Tribune, January 30, 2009.
[6] Ephesians 6:12
[7] John 10:10
[8] Colossians 1:13
[9] Colossians 2:15
[10] Ryan Smith, "2016 Olympics: Did Derrion Albert Beating Footage Kill Chicago's Dream?," CBS News, October 2, 2009.

Chapter Ten

[1] Luke 1:53
[2] Liz Logan, "New mural highlights West Side agency's work among homeless," *Medill Reports Chicago*, August 20, 2008.
[3] Emily Badger, "Greening Vacant Lots Linked to Reduced Gun Violence", The Atlantic City Lab, November, 21, 2011.
[4] Charles Lee, "Beyond Toxic Wastes and Race" in *Confronting Environmental Racism: Voices from the Grassroots*, ed., Robert Bullard (Boston: South End, 1993).
[5] John R. Logan and Harvey Molotch, *Urban Fortunes: The Political Economy of Place*, (Berkeley and Los Angeles: University of California Press, 1987).
[6] Taken from Pilsen Environmental Rights and Reform Organization (P.E.R.R.O.) website: pilsenperro.org/coal-power.
[7] Jeremiah 29:11
[8] 1 Peter 2:9
[9] Romans 8:17
[10] 2 Timothy 2:12

ABOUT THE AUTHOR

Shawn Casselberry is a passionate advocate for God's justice, author, and Executive Director for Mission Year, a national Christian ministry devoted to coming alongside what God is doing in the city by partnering with churches, ministries, leaders, activists, and neighbors who are transforming their communities. For the last decade, Shawn has been a witness to God's grace and transformation in the city of Chicago. As a drum instructor and youth mentor, Shawn is part of a community drumline for youth with incarcerated loved ones. He has a passion for mobilizing the church around issues of racial and economic justice, particularly issues of mass incarceration, immigration, and youth violence. Trained in Kingian non-violence and community organizing, Shawn actively works for peace and reconciliation in the city. As an ordained minister, Shawn speaks all across the country at colleges, churches, and conferences calling people to love God and love people. Shawn has a Masters degree in World Missions and Evangelism from Asbury Theological Seminary and is currently working on a Doctor of Ministry degree in Building Beloved Community from McCormick Theological Seminary. Shawn has been married to his wife Jen for 14 years and lives in the North Lawndale neighborhood on Chicago's west side.

You can contact Shawn or request him to speak at: shawn@missionyear.org. Follow him on Twitter at @scasselberry.

Mission Year is actively looking for passionate, committed single and married young adults ages 18-29 years of age to encounter God in the city. Fall in love with Jesus and the neighborhood. Come alive in your gifts and purpose. Build beloved community across all dividing lines. Become a lifelong advocate for God's justice. Mission Year trains young men and women to be faithful Christian leaders who will transform the church, the city, and the world.

Apply today at: www.missionyear.org/applynow

Bring your college or church group on a Mission Year justice trip to experience what God is doing in the city: info@missionyear.org

Made in the USA
Charleston, SC
06 February 2015